Published by Vision Sports Publishing in 2010

Vision Sports Publishing
19-23 High Street
Kingston upon Thames
Surrey
KT1 1LL

www.visionsp.co.uk

Text © Scott McDermott
Illustrations © Bob Bond Sporting Caricatures

ISBN: 978-1905326-98-3

Editor: Ronnie Esplin
Series editor: Jim Drewett
Series production: Martin Cloake
Design: Neal Cobourne
Illustrations: Bob Bond
Cover photography: Paul Downes, Objective Image
All pictures: Getty Images unless otherwise stated

ted and bound in China by Toppan Printing Co Ltd

gue record for this book is available from the British Library

THIS IS AN UNOFFICIAL PUBLICATION

in The Pocket Book of Rangers are correct up until the end
of the 2009/10 season.

THE
POCKET
OF
RANG

RANGERS

TERRY BUTC

Pri
A CIP catal

By Sc

All statistic

CONTENTS

JOHN BROWN

Signing for Rangers was the best thing that ever happened to me in my life. I had been a supporter of the club in the 1970s and 1980s before becoming a professional footballer myself.

To support Rangers and then go on to play for them during the nine-in-a-row period was a fantastic feeling. It was a great honour for me.

When I was at Hamilton and Dundee there wasn't a thought in my head that one day I'd play for the club I loved.

Getting the opportunity to meet greats like Willie Waddell, Willie Thornton, Jock 'Tiger' Shaw and John Greig was incredible. As was getting to play alongside players like Davie Cooper, Terry Butcher, Ray Wilkins, Paul Gascoigne and Brian Laudrup. That was a real thrill for me.

I'll never forget how the move to Rangers came about. I was playing for Dundee against them on a Wednesday night at Dens Park and they beat us 4–0. But I had a boot at Graeme Souness, which I got a yellow card for. He was on the deck and a few of the Rangers boys were ready to rip my head off. But Souness got up and fended them off.

The next day I got a phone call from him. He told me he wanted someone in his side who was brave enough to have a kick at him. I told him if he could sort it, I'd be there in a flash. I actually got a three-year deal, which was written out by Souness on a beer mat.

I didn't have an agent back then and I wasn't interested in money. I looked upon it as a once-in-a-lifetime opportunity that I had to grab.

I always knew Rangers were a big club but it was only after a number of years there that I realised just how big they are. The fan base around the world is second to none.

What I loved about playing for Rangers was, when we won a game, my folks could go to their work in Glasgow on a Monday morning with their chests puffed out.

I find it a bit embarrassing to be called a Rangers legend. I'm just a punter. I was a welder to trade but I got a chance in life to play for Rangers Football Club and I'm grateful for that.

I was recently at a NARSA (North American Rangers Supporters Association) convention in Las Vegas with Colin Stein and Lorenzo Amoruso.

To be worshipped by the fans over there was humbling – it's nice to know I helped make those people happy during a successful period in Rangers' history.

...CLUB DIRECTORY...

Club address: Rangers Football Club,
Ibrox Stadium, 150 Edmiston Drive,
Glasgow, G51 2XD

General club enquiries: 0871 702 1972

Option 1: Match day and season tickets

Option 2: Hospitality

Option 3: Argyle House restaurant

Option 4: Ibrox Tours

Option 5: General enquiries, soccer schools, young supporters club, travel club, events

Option 6: Rangers JJB retail

Option 7: Follow with pride incident line

Rangers Charity Foundation: 0141 580 8775

Rangers utilities: 0800 408 4321

Rangers megastore at Ibrox: 0141 427 4444

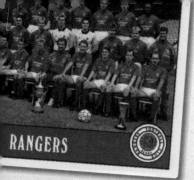

Rangers telephone shopping: 0800 111 4186
General shopping: 0871 641 2295
Rangers soccer schools: 0871 702 1972

EMAIL ADDRESSES:
General enquiries: webmail@rangers.co.uk
Ticket office: ticketcentre@rangers.co.uk
Argyle House restaurant:
argylehouserestaurant@rangers.co.uk
Hospitality: hospitality@rangers.co.uk
Rangers megastore rangersmegastore@jjbsports.com
Bar 72: bar72screening@rangers.co.uk
Rangers soccer schools: soccerschools@rangers.co.uk
Commercial and advertising: advertising@rangers.co.uk
Club website: www.rangers.co.uk

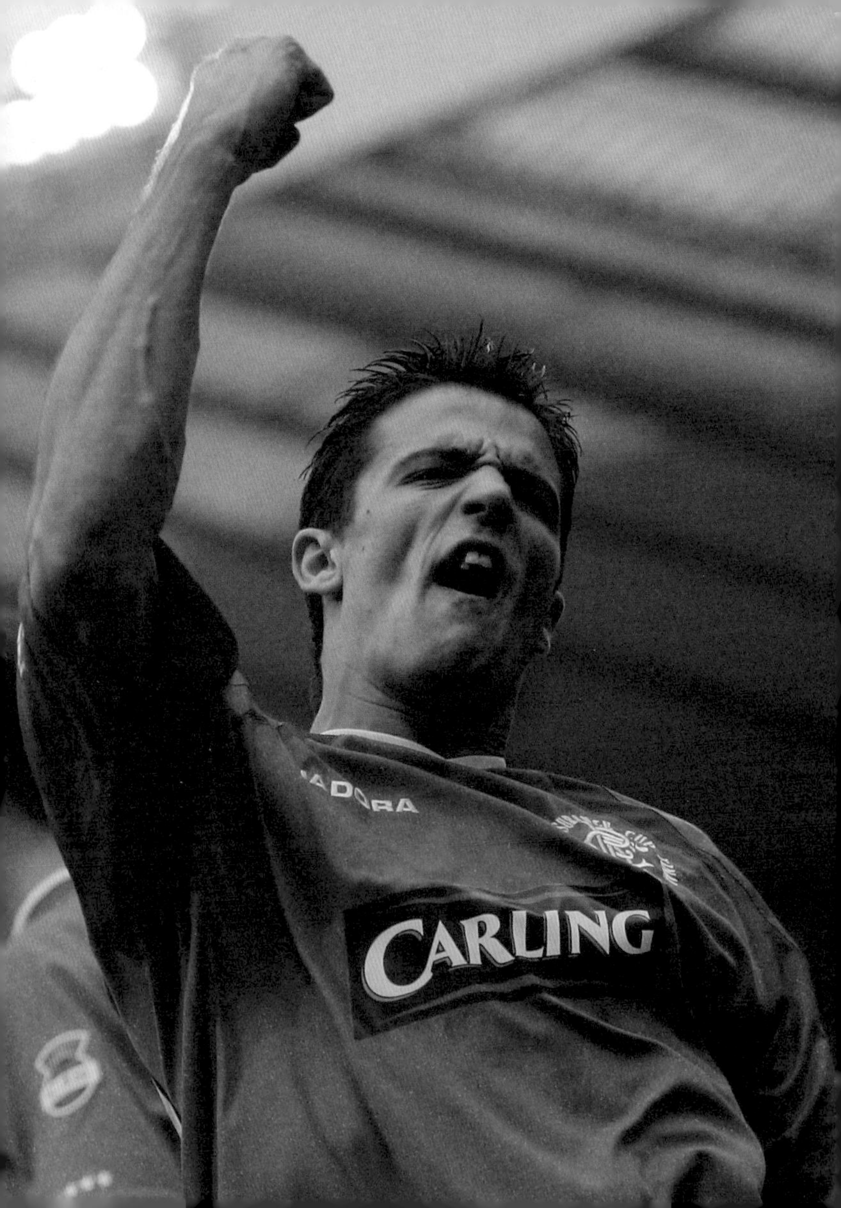
CARLING

THE RANGERS STORY
A GIANT IS BORN
1872-1954

Rangers may have a rich, illustrious, trophy-laden history. But the club was born from humble beginnings in 1872 when four teenagers had the simple idea of forming a football club.

Despite having no money, no kit, no ball and no pitch of their own, Peter McNeil, brother Moses, Peter Campbell and William McBeath were determined to turn their dream into reality.

Their first match against Callander FC at Flesher's Haugh on Glasgow Green was open to all spectators, as it was a public park. The boys had to be there first just to get the pitch. The newly-formed home team wore their street clothes, with the exception of a few 'ringers' who had their own strips because they had been signed by other clubs in the area.

A second-hand ball was used as the teams battled out a 0-0 draw but the scoreline didn't matter – Rangers Football Club had been born. No one could have predicted the glory and success which would follow in the next century and more as Rangers became a Scottish football institution renowned and admired across the globe.

Their name was taken from an English rugby club and by their second fixture – an 11-0 win over Clyde – they were wearing the now-famous light blue jerseys.

It was the following year before office bearers were elected, training sessions were organised and a friendly fixture list drawn up. It was a family club in

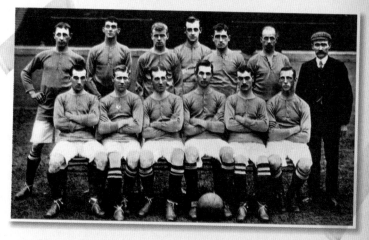

One of the earliest pictures of a Rangers team, taken in the 1905/06 season

that Moses and Peter McNeil were joined by brother Hugh; two more Campbells, John and James, got into the starting line-up and both Tom and Alexander Vallance also shone.

By 1876 Rangers had their first international player when Moses McNeil made his Scotland debut in a 4-0 victory over Wales, a year before the Gers lost to Vale of Leven in the Scottish Cup final.

It was 1891 before the club could celebrate its first domestic honour when they enjoyed a magnificent season in the newly-created Scottish League Championship. By then they had moved to Ibrox from Kinning Park and, after winning 13 of their 18 matches, the title was shared with Dumbarton.

Their first Scottish Cup success came at the third time of asking in 1894 when – after losing two

Rangers in action at Ibrox in 1934

previous finals – they beat Old Firm rivals Celtic 3-1. Rangers were on their way to the summit of Scottish football.

Under the guidance of the club's first manager, William Wilton, the club were performing well and in season 1898/99 they achieved a feat which hasn't been matched by any side in the world to this day.

Captain George Young, seen here with the Scottish Cup, was a key member of the great team of the late 1940s

Rangers won every game of their league campaign, scoring 79 goals and conceding just 18, to win the championship ahead of closest rivals Hearts who were ten points adrift.

But Celtic denied them Scottish Cup glory by winning 2-0 in the final. Incredibly, Wilton's side would wait 29 years to do the double.

Rangers became a limited company in March 1899, with a board of directors led by chairman James Henderson. Even at that point, the club had come a long way from that first friendly game on the Glasgow

Green. Later that year they moved to the new Ibrox and their progression off the field was paying dividends on it, as they retained their title for three years.

Their joy turned to sadness, though, in 1902 when the first of the Ibrox disasters took place during a Scotland v England international match. When part of the terracing collapsed, 25 people lost their lives and another 500 were injured.

By 1914, a man by the name of William Struth had joined the club as a trainer. He would go on to become an Ibrox legend by leading Rangers to unprecedented success.

Wilton and Struth began a period of Rangers domination that lasted until 1939 but tragically the club's first boss wouldn't get to enjoy a run which saw the club win 15 titles in 21 years. In 1920, a day after the title was won, he drowned in a boating accident.

Struth took over, managing the club for 34 years and winning 18 championships, ten Scottish Cups and two League Cups – making him the most successful Rangers gaffer in history.

In 1928 he masterminded the club's first double in historic fashion. They clinched the title and followed it up with a stunning 4-0 win over Celtic in the Scottish Cup final at Hampden – the first time they'd lifted the trophy since 1903.

As Struth's team set the Scottish game alight there were few disappointments but in 1932 they were devastated to score a record number of league goals – 118 – yet finish runners-up to champions Motherwell.

But just two years later they clinched their second double. No one could compete with Rangers in the 1930s when it came to lifting silverware and fans flocked to Ibrox from all over.

On 2nd January 1939 the biggest crowd ever at a match in the United Kingdom – 118,567 – watched goals from Dave Kinnear and Alex Venters give the home side a 2-1 win over Old Firm rivals Celtic.

Struth's side continued to excel during the war years, lifting various titles including the Summer Cup and the Victory Cup. Several Ibrox stalwarts were involved in active service during the war including legendary figure Willie Thornton, who won the Military Medal for his Army efforts in Sicily.

Just before the Scottish League resumed after the Second World War, a special match at Ibrox took place against the then relatively unknown Russian outfit Moscow Dynamo. A crowd of 95,000 people watched Torry Gillick and George Young secure a 2-2 draw.

The immediate post-war era became famous in Rangers folklore due to the club's indestructable 'Iron Curtain' defence which underpinned the winning of the treble for the first time.

The League Cup was introduced to the Scottish game in 1946/47 and a Struth-led Gers won the inaugural final 4-0 against Aberdeen. They also collected the first post-war title – the long-serving boss was simply carrying on from where he'd left off.

In 1948/49, the treble was won. A victory over Raith Rovers in the League Cup final was followed up by a Scottish Cup final win over Clyde. The championship was closely contested by Dundee who threw it away on the last day of the campaign, allowing Rangers to capitalise and make history.

Sadly, Struth's health was deteriorating. After two trophyless seasons, he somehow got his side motivated to clinch one last title in 1953 when they were crowned champions on goal difference.

But after helping the club to 30 major trophies, he stood down from the Ibrox hot seat and was replaced by Scot Symon.

Willie Waddell slots home a penalty against Celtic in 1949

THE CLUB CREST

The Rangers Football Club crest is
instantly recognised and acknowledged all over the
world. Wherever you go, that famous 'RFC' scroll will
be seen somewhere on a royal blue shirt or shorts –
in a bar, restaurant or on television.

The lion motif was widely used from the 1950s onwards

Those three letters, woven together, are the symbol of
Rangers and the specific design is believed to have
been used by the club since its formation in 1872. But
the oldest item found to carry the iconic Gers badge is
from the 1881/82 season. It is stamped in gold on 'The
Member's Ticket', which was used at one of Rangers'
early home grounds, Kinning Park – the venue used by
the club before their move to Ibrox.

'The Member's Ticket', which also features the words Rangers Football Club above the crest, is now on display in the famous Ibrox trophy room alongside other treasured, historical items linked to the club's illustrious past.

It's widely believed the traditional 'RFC' scroll design remained in place at Rangers for more than 70 years. But in 1959 Rangers decided to move away from this particular style and detail, replacing it with a lion and the now famous Rangers motto 'Ready'.

It's believed the original motto was 'Aye Ready Aye' which was later cut to 'Aye Ready' then to just 'Ready' in 1966.

Classic shirt, classic crest

This hasn't been confirmed officially by the club but legendary Rangers striker Jim Forrest remembers seeing the words 'Aye Ready' on one side of Ibrox's main stand in the 1960s.

He said: "I used to see 'Aye Ready' but it was changed around the time I was at Rangers. It was always 'Ready' on our club blazers and it was officially changed later. That's stuck and everyone now knows the Rangers motto as 'Ready'.

The circular badge has gone through several incarnations

A new circular shape was also chosen in which the lion was circled by the words 'The Rangers Football Club Ltd'.

But this particular crest didn't last long and was changed again at the end of the 1960s. The club was required to register a new crest with the Scottish League and, like the traditional 'RFC', it would become a symbol immediately identifiable to supporters across the globe.

The 'Ready' motto featured again within a circle design but 'The Rangers Football Club Ltd' was shortened to 'Rangers Football Club' on the outer rim of the new-look badge. In the centre a large football was used instead of the lion, with 'Ready' becoming far more prominent as the club's official slogan. This has remained the case ever since.

Although the 'RFC' scroll was temporarily ditched in 1959, it made a welcome return nine years later when it featured on the club's new round-necked home shirt for the first time in its history. It was added to the team shorts a decade later for the start of the 1978/79 season, where it remains.

Over the years, there have been small changes and

alterations to the scroll crest on the club's kit – both home and away.

From 1990 to 1994, the 'Rangers Football Club' and 'Ready' motto were placed above and below the 'RFC' crest on the club's Admiral and Adidas shirts as Gers began their charge towards nine league titles in a row under Walter Smith.

In 1997/98 – Smith's last season in his original spell at Ibrox – the crest was situated within a small shield in what was Nike's first year in partnership with the club.

But perhaps the most significant change to the Rangers crest came at the beginning of the 2003/04 campaign when Alex McLeish was manager.

Having just clinched their 50th league championship and secured a domestic treble, it was decided that five stars would be added above the 'RFC' scroll crest – one for every ten titles won by Rangers in their history.

These stars have remained there ever since and having just secured their 53rd league flag under Smith in May 2010, it's unlikely to be too long before a sixth star is added to the famous Rangers jersey.

Michael Mols wears the 5-star shirt with pride

BARCELONA BEARS

R.F.C. 3
MOSCOW DYNAMO 2
BARCELONA

MAY
24
1972

MCCLOY   CONN
JARDINE   MCLEAN
MATHIESON   D.JOHNSTONE
GREIG   SMITH
STEIN   MACDONALD
W. JOHNSTONE 2

Willie Waddell's sole task in season 1971/72 was to try and lift his squad out of the grief and depression which had engulfed them during the time of the Ibrox Disaster just months earlier.

Rangers players had been ordered by their manager to attend every one of the 66 funerals in honour of the people who had lost their lives in the tragedy.

He knew it would be difficult to raise them on both the domestic and European front. That's why no one, even those within Ibrox, could have envisaged the season ending in glory at the Nou Camp in Barcelona.

The previous year had been spent immersed in sadness and Rangers had finished a disappointing fourth in the league, despite winning the League Cup. And they didn't start the 71/72 term in any better form. They lost four of their opening five league games, which included a 3-2 defeat to Celtic.

They'd also been beaten by their Old Firm rivals twice in their League Cup section before the end of August.

By the following May they had to settle for third place in the championship, having lost 11 of their 34 matches. But

Rangers excelled on the European stage as the Barcelona Bears were born.

French side Stade Rennes were their first opponents in the Cup-Winner's Cup and after a 1-1 away-leg result, Waddell's men went through after a 1-0 victory in Glasgow.

Against Sporting Lisbon Rangers took a 3-2 advantage to Portugal, after going three clear, and lost by the same margin in an epic return leg.

Sporting had won 4-3 after extra-time, leveling it at 6-6 on aggregate. The game went to penalties, which the Portuguese side won, leaving Rangers believing they were out.

But a Scottish journalist pointed out to Waddell that UEFA's rule book stated away goals counted as double even after 90 minutes and it was, in fact, the Ibrox side who should progress.

Dutch referee Laurens van Raavens quickly realised his error and admitted the game shouldn't have gone to a penalty shoot-out – Rangers were through.

Waddell was using the European competition to tinker with his team, experimenting with players in unfamiliar positions and basing his side on youth, with a view to the future.

Italian outfit Torino were Rangers' opponents in the quarter-final. The home side were shocked in Turin as Willie Johnston grabbed the opening goal. The first leg

Top: Willie Johnstone celebrates his opener. Above: Front page news

finished 1-1 but it gave Rangers a decent chance in the return game at Ibrox. A solitary Alex MacDonald strike sealed the tie to set up a mouthwatering semi-final clash with German giants Bayern Munich.

Bayern were led by legendary figure Franz Beckenbauer but Rangers held

The trophy was presented in a room inside the Nou Camp…

on in Munich albeit it desperately at times. Paul Breitner broke the deadlock as the Germans dominated the first half but Gers improved after the break and Colin Stein's cross was knocked in by Rainer Zobel for a priceless own goal.

At Ibrox, Beckenbauer and his Bayern team-mates were rocked by the electric atmosphere. Sandy Jardine scored a magnificent goal in the first minute and teenager Derek Parlane, taking over from the injured John Greig, grabbed a second before half time to book a place in the Cup-Winner's Cup final for the third time in the club's history.

They had lost on their two previous appearances – to Fiorentina in 1961 and to old foes Bayern Munich six years later. But Rangers' and Waddell's time had come.

They faced Moscow Dynamo in the final on 24th May 1972 and by half-time they had raced into a two-goal lead thanks to Stein's bullet shot and Johnston's deft header. Johnston added a third early in the second half, from a Peter McCloy punt, and the Gers fans began to celebrate.

But complacency and tiredness kicked in and Dynamo staged a comeback.

When the Russians, still in mid-season while the Scots had finished weeks earlier, made it 3-2 with three minutes remaining, the tension was unbearable.

But Waddell's men hung on to clinch their first-ever European trophy. They had finally emulated rivals Celtic by getting their hands on continental silverware after the Hoops' European Cup success of 1967.

Understandably, the travelling army of Rangers supporters were overwhelmed by joy but their invading of the Barcelona pitch was to prove costly. Spanish riot police got heavy-handed and there were ugly clashes with Scots fans.

Sadly, Rangers captain Greig was prevented from lifting the trophy in public and was instead ushered into a room within the Nou Camp to be presented with the cup by UEFA officials.

The pitch invasion also earned the club a two-year ban from Europe (later reduced to one on appeal) so Greig and his team-mates weren't given the chance to defend their title the following season.

They did, however, parade the trophy around a rain-soaked Ibrox shortly after arriving back in Glasgow as fans finally clapped eyes on the prize.

Just weeks later, Waddell, having achieved what he set out to do, stepped down as manager.

... after jubilant Rangers fans swarmed on to the pitch

RANGERS
COMIC STRIP HISTORY
1

1987...IN AN EXPLOSIVE OLD FIRM DERBY, RANGERS 'KEEPER CHRIS WOODS IS SENT OFF. FANS FAVOURITE GRAHAM ROBERTS HAS TO GO IN GOAL, AND BY HALF-TIME CELTIC ARE 2-0 AHEAD...

GASP... HE'S SAVED ANOTHER ONE!

RANGERS SHOULD BE DEAD AND BURIED BY NOW...

ROBERTS KEEPS HIS TEAM IN IT...

TERRY BUTCHER IS ALSO DISMISSED, BUT ALLY McCOIST PULLS A GOAL BACK, AND WITH THE FANS SINGING THEIR HEADS OFF...

GOAL!

RICHARD GOUGH!

THE NINE MEN HAVE EQUALISED!

IT WAS THE VERY LAST MINUTE!

AS HE AND A RANGERS DEFENDER KEPT PASSING THE BALL TO EACH OTHER TO PRESERVE A PRECIOUS POINT, STAND-IN GOALIE ROBERTS WAS CONDUCTING THE IBROX CROWD AS IF THEY WERE AN ORCHESTRA...

IBROX
STADIUM

The iconic red brick facade of the main stand at Ibrox is famous around the globe and is now one of Glasgow's listed buildings.

But the current UEFA five-star stadium is a far cry from the humble beginnings of Rangers FC and their first home at Fleshers Haugh on Glasgow Green. That's where the club played their inaugural match in 1872.

Just three years later they moved to a field in Burnbank in Glasgow, gaining a credible 1-1 draw in their first match against Vale of Leven on 11 September 1875.

Within the first year at Burnbank Gers had moved again, this time to Kinning Park a mile or so from Ibrox. Their opening fixture at the Clydesdale ground on 2nd September 1876 was against Vale of Leven again but this time they chalked up a 2-1 victory.

At that time, Rangers could attract crowds of around 2,000 but they didn't own the land their ground stood on and so were forced to relocate again in 1887. Their last game at this venue was a resounding win over Old Westminsters, beaten 5-1 in the FA Cup quarter-finals.

The club played their remaining fixtures that season at Cathkin Park, home of the now defunct Third Lanark FC, before moving to Govan and the original Ibrox.

Their new home was situated where Edmiston House currently sits – just yards from Ibrox Stadium.

The huge pitch was surrounded by a running track and boasted a pavillion, dressing rooms with baths, and a committee room.

A grandstand holding 1,200 people was erected and the opening match against English giants Preston North End on 20th August 1887 drew 18,000 fans to the 15,000 capacity ground. Supporters spilled on to the pitch and the match was abandoned after 70 minutes with North End leading 8-1.

Here, Rangers would share their first-ever league title with Dumbarton in 1890/91. They won the championship outright in 1898/99 with what

An illustration of Ibrox in 1902, at the time of the first disaster (see page 152)

remains to this day the only 100 per cent league record ever achieved in world football.

In that season the club became a limited liability company with the aim of raising funds for a new, bigger ground. They didn't have to move far, just the short distance to the site of where Ibrox stands today.

Their first match at the stadium was a 2-1 win over Hearts in the Inter-City League on 30th December 1899.

Soon a grandstand housing 4,500 fans was built and with another stand, which became known as 'The Bovril Stand' because of the giant advert for the drink on its roof, it meant Rangers now boasted two covered enclosures.

Around £20,000 had been spent on the new Ibrox, a vast sum at that time, and the capacity increased to 75,000. Behind each goal were scaffolded terraces made of huge planks on iron frames. Because of the ground's capacity, Ibrox was chosen to host a Scotland v England clash in 1902.

But tragically it resulted in what was the first Ibrox disaster when one of the wooden terraces collapsed and 26 people lost their lives.

It was decided that solid earth banking would provide a far safer base at either end of the ground and the capacity was cut to 25,000.

Renowned construction engineer Archibald Leitch, a Rangers fan, was recruited by the club. He had already worked on Hampden Park and Celtic Park. By 1910, Ibrox had taken on a new bowl-like

Huge crowds would turn up for Old Firm derbies... such as this one in 1957

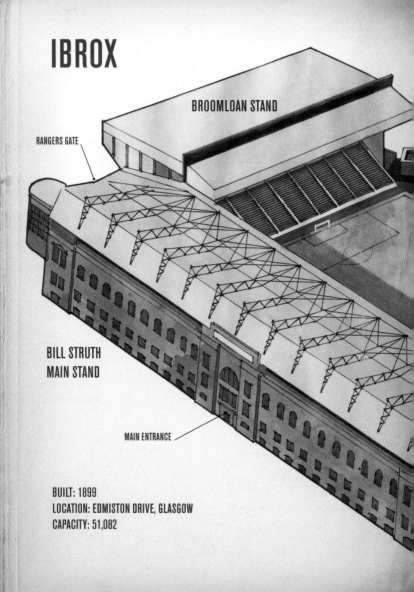

IBROX

BROOMLOAN STAND

RANGERS GATE

**BILL STRUTH
MAIN STAND**

MAIN ENTRANCE

BUILT: 1899
LOCATION: EDMISTON DRIVE, GLASGOW
CAPACITY: 51,082

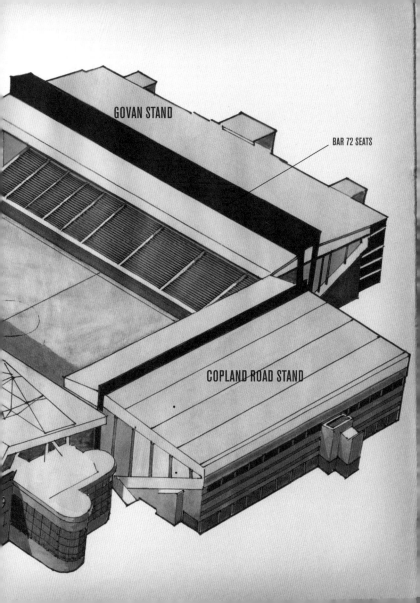

GOVAN STAND

BAR 72 SEATS

COPLAND ROAD STAND

shape and had expanded to accommodate 63,000 fans. After the First World War the capacity was up to 80,000.

The centrepiece was Leitch's magnificent grandstand which included the club's offices, dressing-rooms, kit room and the now-famous marble staircase. It was officially opened before the

New Year match against Celtic in 1929 and Gers celebrated by hammering their Old Firm rivals 3-0.

The gates between the Main and Broomloan Stands

This was a hugely successful time. Five straight Scottish title wins meant Rangers were attracting huge crowds and on 2nd January 1939, 118,566 turned up to see them beat Celtic 2-1 – still a record attendance for a British league match.

There were no structural changes to the stadium in the next 30 years but legislation limited the capacity to 80,000. It was another Old Firm game in 1971 which impacted on the future of Ibrox Stadium forever.

When 66 people died on Staircase 13 at the end of a match with Celtic following a crush, Willie Waddell put forward his vision for an all-seated stadium. He visited Dortmund in Germany to see a similar project and started the work which resulted in the modern-day Ibrox.

In 1973 bench seats were fitted as a temporary measure along the north side of the ground, and the stand named the Centenary Stand. Just five years later, the east terracing was ripped up and replaced by the all-seated Copland Road Stand. A similar stand, the Broomloan Road Stand, was erected at the opposite end of the stadium. By 1981 the Centenary Stand had been demolished and replaced by the Govan Stand seating 10,300.

In the decade following the Ibrox disaster the sum of £10 million had been spent to ensure such tragedy was never repeated.

The pace of change intensified when David Murray took over as chairman in 1988 and in his first ten years at the helm, £52 million was spent on redevelopment.

The Club Deck was added to the Bill Struth Main Stand in 1991, with both old standing enclosures filled with seats. When the corners between the Broomloan Road, Govan and Copland Road stands were filled in with seats, as well as the introduction of Bar 72 in 2006, the capacity was set at 51,082. The detail of Leitch's red-brick masterpiece have been retained within the modern glass and steel structure.

Ibrox has also hosted concerts by the likes of Frank Sinatra, Elton John and Rod Stewart and, in 1980, Scottish boxer Jim Watt defended his world

lightweight title there against Howard Davis.

Legendary figure Waddell would have been proud that his vision of Ibrox has been realised. It is one of few stadia in Europe to be awarded five-star status by UEFA and boasts the very best of facilities for fans and corporate guests from around the world.

Ibrox is now a stadium fit for the 21st century but which retains its heritage

GREAT GOALS

DAVIE COOPER
1979 DRYBROUGH CUP FINAL V CELTIC

The greatest-ever Rangers goal. Davie Cooper would have been proud of that accolade.

His wonderful, audacious finish against Celtic in the 1979 Drybrough Cup Final at Hampden was voted the best in the club's history after a worldwide poll of supporters. Quite simply, it typified Cooper as a player. Skilful, cheeky, nonchalant, breathtaking. The real shame is that there is only one camera angle of it and it can't be fully savoured in all its glory. Thankfully, Cooper's goal will remain long in the memory.

Back to goal, just inside Celtic's 18-yard-box, he appeared to have nowhere to go as he was surrounded by defenders. But it was as if Cooper had the ball attached to his left-foot on a string. He lofted it over four Celtic defenders who couldn't get near him. Here was Cooper playing 'keepy-uppy' on his own in front of more than 60,000 fans.

If his skill in getting into that position was sublime, his finish was mesmeric. Mere mortals would have smashed the ball into the net from seven yards out, but not Cooper.

He coolly controlled the ball on his chest before side-footing it past on-rushing Celtic goalkeeper Peter Latchford and into the bottom corner.

When Cooper died in 1995, a Scottish TV documentary played the Queen song *It's a Kind of Magic* over footage of Cooper's goals. None was more magical than this one.

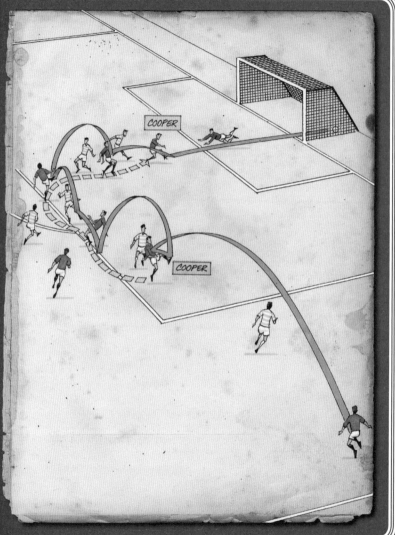

COOPER

COOPER

ROBERT FLECK
1986 UEFA CUP
FIRST ROUND
V ILVES TAMPERE

Robert Fleck scored Rangers' third goal against Ilves Tampere at Ibrox in 1986 to complete a fantastic hat-trick.

But ask any Gers fan about their memories of that night and there will only be one name on their lips – Davie Cooper.

Fleck may have knocked the ball into the back of the Finns' net but it was legendary winger Cooper who mesmerised the Tampere defence and laid it on a plate for the young striker.

Rangers had been knocked out at the first round stage of the UEFA Cup the previous season and were determined not to fall at the first hurdle again. Fleck and Cooper made sure of that as Rangers ran out easy 4-0 winners in the first-leg tie.

Already two-nil up, Coop picked the ball up on the left flank and went on one of his trademark mazy runs. The Ibrox crowd were lifted off their seats as he waltzed past four bemused defenders and drove into the box.

As a fifth Tampere player tried to close him down, he shaped to shoot but fooled him and the Finnish keeper by squaring it to Fleck ten yards out who rolled it into an empty net.

It sealed Fleck's hat-trick and Rangers' passage into the next round - but the goal was all about the genius of Cooper.

ALLY MCCOIST
1992 EUROPEAN CUP SECOND ROUND V LEEDS UNITED

It's rare that any Rangers goal is greeted with eery silence. But at Elland Road in 1992, you could have heard a pin drop after Ally McCoist struck to secure the Ibrox club's place in the first-ever group stage of the Champions League

There were no away fans allowed at either leg of a mammoth tie dubbed The Battle of Britain. So when McCoist's header nestled in John Lukic's net to seal a memorable victory, the home support were stunned. Not just by the fact their side had been knocked out by the Scottish champions – but by the sheer quality of the goal.

With Rangers 1-0 up thanks to a Mark Hateley goal and 3-1 ahead on aggregate, Ibrox stalwart Ian Ferguson broke up a Leeds attack and sent his side away on the break.

Mark Hateley's deft backheel found Ian Durrant on the left flank who then sent Hateley galloping down the wing with a measured pass. The big Englishman took a touch before producing a sublime cross for his strike partner who dived to head home from six yards out.

A shattered McCoist ran to celebrate but, realising there were no Gers fans present, simply sunk to his knees in delight.

Legendary commentator Brian Moore summed up the goal and Walter Smith's side's performance that night by saying: "Rangers, now, have thoroughly killed off this European tie."

DURRANT

HATELEY

DURRANT

HATELEY

HATELEY

McCOIST

PAUL GASCOIGNE
1996 SCOTTISH PREMIER LEAGUE V ABERDEEN

Paul Gascoigne always did have the ability to win a game on his own.

But that was never more evident than when he single-handedly won Rangers their eighth consecutive SPL title with a stunning hat-trick against Aberdeen. The importance of winning that particular championship should never be under-estimated as it put Gers within one trophy of equalling Celtic's haul of nine in a row. If they'd have fallen at eight – a remarkable achievement in itself – it would still have been seen as a failure.

Rangers needed a victory on a gorgeous sunny day in 1996 but were dealt a huge blow when the Dons took an early lead. Walter Smith needed an inspiration and Gazza delivered.

His first goal that day was terrific. A trademark step-over and dribble on the edge of the box before a cool finish high into Michael Watt's net.

But it's his second strike which will go down in Ibrox folklore. He picked up Alan McLaren's interception in his own half and drove towards Aberdeen's goal. Gascoigne ran a full 60 yards, shrugging off challenges from Paul Bernard and Stewart McKimmie, before calmly placing the ball past Watt.

It was maverick Gazza at his best. Pace, power, control and a devastating finish to score one of Gers' all-time great goals.

Ibrox erupted as he ran to celebrate before being swamped by his team-mates. He wasn't finished there, either, as he slotted home a late penalty to bag a hat-trick, the match ball and eight in a row.

MCLAREN

GASCOIGNE

GASCOIGNE

BRIAN LAUDRUP
1997 SCOTTISH PREMIER LEAGUE V DUNDEE UNITED

Danish superstar Brian Laudrup had never scored a headed goal for Rangers. Charlie Miller had only ever used his left leg to stand on. But incredibly, in 1997, that combination of unlikely events sealed one of the most famous victories in the club's history.

The feat of 'nine in a row' was the Holy Grail for Rangers fans — it would equal Celtic's record of nine league titles on the trot and put an end to decades of gloating from Hoops supporters. At Tannadice on a summer Wednesday night, Walter Smith's side needed a victory to seal the ninth consecutive championship and cement their name in the history books.

Laudrup provided the decisive goal with a bullet header which will live long in the memory of every Ibrox fan.

Just 11 minutes into the match, full back Davie Robertson took a quick throw in which sent Miller scampering down the left. He swung his left boot at the ball on the half volley and sent over a delicious cross that was met flush on the forehead by Laudrup.

Like an experienced target man, the cultured winger gave Dundee United keeper Sieb Dykstra no chance with a header that flew into the top corner and "set the stadium alight" in the words of commentator Jock Brown.

Laudrup has taken his place in the Rangers Hall of Fame and his goal to seal 'nine in a row' will never be forgotten.

LAUDRUP

MILLER

ROBERTSON

PETER LOVENKRANDS
2002 SCOTTISH CUP
FINAL V CELTIC

To score the winning goal against Celtic at any time is a dream come true for any Rangers player. To do it in the Scottish Cup final at Hampden, in the last minute? Well, it just doesn't get any better than that.

That's why when Peter Lovenkrands did just that in 2002 to seal a memorable 3-2 win over their Old Firm rivals, he leapt straight over the advertising boards to celebrate with the jubilant Gers fans.

It was a game which ebbed and flowed, one which will go down as a modern day classic. Twice Rangers had to come from behind after Celtic goals from John Hartson and Bobo Balde. But Alex McLeish's side had resilience. Lovenkrands and skipper Barry Ferguson had both hit equalisers and in the dying seconds of the match it was set up for someone to become a hero.

The Danish striker grabbed that opportunity. Rangers had won possession in midfield and left winger Neil McCann set off down the flank. He conjured up a teasing cross between the Hoops' back line and keeper Rab Douglas who didn't know whether to come off his line or stay.

Lovenkrands didn't hesitate. He got free of his marker and launched himself at the ball. His diving header wrong-footed Douglas and nestled in the bottom corner – sending the Rangers fans into a state of delirium behind the goal.

There was no time for Celtic to hit back as Lovenkrands ensured the cup was coming back to Ibrox.

AMORUSO

McCANN

McCANN

LOVENKRANDS

KENNY MILLER
2010 SCOTTISH LEAGUE CUP FINAL V ST MIRREN

"We only need nine men" was the chant from the Rangers crowd at Hampden.

Against all the odds and in the face of adversity, the light blues had just won another League Cup thanks to a solitary Kenny Miller goal.

St Mirren were the opponents for the 2010 final and Walter Smith's side weren't at their best. The Paisley outfit were the better team and Gers' bid to lift the trophy looked doomed when Kevin Thomson and Danny Wilson were sent off in the second half.

With the score still at 0-0, Gers had to show all the resilience and determination they had become renowned for that season. The Buddies tried to capitalise on their two-man advantage but Rangers battled to keep them at bay.

St Mirren should have known never to write off Rangers and with just ten minutes left Miller scored a sensational winner.

Davie Weir broke up a St Mirren attack on the edge of his own box, stepped out of defence and passed the ball out wide to sub Steven Naismith. With fresh legs, he carried it deep into Saints' half before picking out the perfect cross for Miller on the run.

His downward header arrowed past keeper Paul Gallagher into the bottom corner and prompted wild celebrations among the Rangers support. The nine men had just put them on cloud nine.

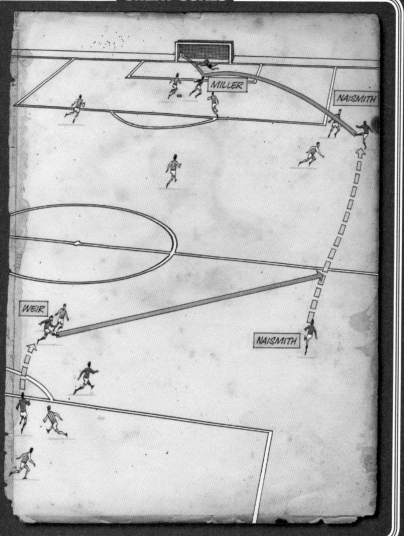

MILLER

NAISMITH

NAISMITH

WEIR

SOUNESS REVOLUTION

Graeme Souness didn't just revolutionise Rangers Football Club. He transformed the whole of Scottish football.

His five-year period at the club will go down as one of the most important in Gers' history as he brought them back to life after a spell in the doldrums.

Souness had been ushered in the back door of Ibrox and unveiled as the new player-manager just 48 hours after the legendary Jock Wallace had been sacked.

Wallace's second spell in charge was bleak and in 1985/86 the team were a lowly fifth in the Premier Division. Gers hadn't won the title in eight years and Ibrox attendances had dropped as low as 12,731 for a January league match against Clydebank.

Months earlier, the club had been taken over by US-based businessman Lawrence Marlborough, who had appointed David Holmes as managing director. Holmes later claimed the idea of appointing 33-year-old Souness

Terry Butcher and Chris Woods were enticed to Rangers by...

had come to him in a dream but, in truth, the wheels had been set in motion by then chairman John Paton.

The former Liverpool legend was with Italian side Sampdoria and preparing for the 1986 World Cup in Mexico when Gers came calling. After meetings with Holmes in London and Milan, the deal was done while Wallace was still at the helm in Glasgow.

When he was finally introduced at Ibrox, Souness dropped one of the biggest hints yet that he would shake the club to its core by going against their Protestant traditions and signing Roman Catholics.

He said: "Signing Catholics isn't a thorny question. I have discussed it with David Holmes. How could I possibly be in this job if I had been told I could not sign a Catholic? After all, I'm married to one."

Souness had the backing of Holmes and Marlborough and there was money to spend on players. He knew the English market well and took advantage of UEFA's ban on English clubs in Europe following the Heysel Stadium disaster.

He enticed goalkeeper Chris Woods to Ibrox and England captain Terry Butcher followed in a sensational move that stunned Scottish football.

In his first season, Souness set out to put Rangers on top of the pile again and he achieved his goal. Despite a controversial start

... Graeme Souness, who could promise European football when English clubs were banned

Souness and Ally
McCoist celebrate
Skol Cup victory
with a young fan
in 1990

to life as player-manager – he was sent off in disgrace at against Hibs on the opening day of the campaign – he brought instant success to Rangers.

After capturing the Glasgow Cup with a win against Celtic at the end of 1985/86 the Light Blues won the League Cup final against the Hoops months into Souness's first full campaign.

After losing just five of their 43 league matches, Gers were crowned champions when Butcher's header sealed the title in a 1-1 draw against Aberdeen at Pittodrie.

His recruitment of big-name stars from England, as well as his own reputation, had given Rangers and Scottish football a higher profile in the UK and abroad.

The following year, though, the Ibrox side struggled to maintain momentum and injuries to key players like Butcher resulted in a poor season.

Celtic were champions in their centenary year but 1988/89 would kick-start one of the most successful spells in Rangers history. It was the first league championship of their glorious nine-in-a-row run.

Souness continued to recruit from England and the likes of Gary Stevens, Kevin Drinkell, Mark Walters and Richard Gough all arrived for big money.

New owner David Murray had taken over the club and was more than willing to back Souness in his quest for domestic domination.

Rangers secured the League Cup with a victory over Aberdeen and won the title thanks to results like the 5-1 demolition of Celtic at Ibrox. They were denied a domestic treble when they lost 1-0 to Celtic in the 1989 Scottish Cup final.

That summer, Mo Johnston walked through the Blue Room doors at Ibrox. A self-confessed Celtic fan and a Roman Catholic, Johnston had agreed to return to Parkhead from French club Nantes. But in a dramatic u-turn, Johnston changed his mind to sign for Rangers in the most controversial transfer ever witnessed in the Scottish game.

It divided the Rangers support, but Souness convinced them it was the right move. Johnston's signing broke down barriers at Ibrox and it is no longer an issue.

The player endeared himself to the majority of fans with a late winning goal against Celtic at Ibrox.

Gers clinched the title in 89/90 but, just before the end of the following campaign, Souness announced he would be leaving to manage Liverpool. To this day, he regrets that decision.

His assistant, Walter Smith, took over the reigns and went on to clinch a record-equalling nine-in-a-row. Despite Souness's walk-out and his various run-ins with authority during his time in Glasgow it's widely accepted he had a hugely positive impact on Rangers and the Scottish game.

Souness's signing of Mo Johnston marked a turning point for the club

RANGERS
COMIC STRIP HISTORY
2

AFTER A SINGLE GOAL DEFEAT AT PARKHEAD, RANGERS CAPTAIN TERRY BUTCHER GOT ANGRY WITH THE REFEREE...

YOU MADE SOME @*⚡*! CRAZY DECISIONS, REF... YOU GAVE THEM EVERYTHING AND US *⚡@⚡! NOTHING!

YOU'RE A @⚡*!⚡! DISGRACE!

BUTCHER KICKED THE NEAREST THING TO HIM, UNAWARE OF THE FACT THAT CELTIC BOSS BILLY MCNEILL WAS BEING INTERVIEWED FOR TV...

I THINK WE DESERVED IT...WHOOOA!

NEXT DAY, DESPITE RANGERS' DEFEAT, BUTCHER WAS APPLAUDED INTO HIS LOCAL PUB... HIS RANT AND HIS ANGRY KICK HAD BEEN SHOWN ON TV!

BEST SHOT OF THE DAY, TERRY!

THE RANGERS STORY
HOME AND AWAY
1954-72

Scot Symon had become just the third manager in Rangers' history when he took on the enviable task of replacing Bill Struth. He needed time to rebuild his squad but managed to do so while winning silverware.

He would win six titles in his time at Ibrox – including a glorious treble in 1964 – with a line-up which still trips off the tongue of most Rangers fans even now. Ritchie, Shearer, Caldow, Greig, McKinnon, Baxter, Henderson, McMillan, Miller, Brand and Wilson are rhymed off in the same way Celtic supporters talk about the Lisbon Lions.

In that treble year, Gers won 25 of their 34 league games, lifted the League Cup after a 5-0 victory over Morton in the final and the Scottish Cup following a thrilling 3-1 triumph against a quality Dundee side at Hampden.

Symon's start to life as Rangers manager, though, had been difficult, especially after the harsh life-ban handed out to Willie Woodburn by the Scottish Football Association. The big defender had head-butted a Stirling Albion player.

However, players such as Jimmy Millar, Alex Scott and Sammy Baird were introduced and didn't let anyone at Ibrox down. Scott scored the goal against Aberdeen in 1956 which secured yet another title.

Rangers retained the championship the following season and, incredibly, Old Firm rivals Celtic helped them to three-in-a-row in 1959. Symon's side just

Queues build up for a 1957 Old Firm derby

needed a point against the Dons on the last day of the campaign but, after a 2-1 defeat, they were booed off the pitch by angry supporters who thought they had blown it.

Celtic just needed to beat Hearts but suffered a 2-1 loss and handed the flag to Gers for the 31st time in the club's history.

A great Hearts side beat them to the title in 1960 but Symon's side lifted the Scottish Cup by virtue of a 4-1 replay win over Celtic. That summer Symon

pulled off a transfer which signalled a period of Rangers dominance over their Glasgow neighbours – as Jim Baxter arrived from Raith Rovers for £17,500.

Baxter would go on to become a Rangers icon and he inspired them to League Cup success in his first season with a win over Kilmarnock – then managed by a certain Willie Waddell, another light blue legend.

The Ayrshire side were Gers' main challengers for the title but after Baxter and co had hammered Celtic 5-1 at Parkhead a few months earlier, they pipped Killie for the championship by a single point.

In 1961 Rangers also made history when they became the first British club to reach a European final. But they lost out to Italian club Fiorentina 4-1 on aggregate in the Cup-Winner's Cup final.

A year later Baxter was at the centre of more cup success as they beat Hearts to the League Cup and St Mirren in the Scottish Cup – but the league was conceded

Action from the 1967 European Cup-Winners' Cup final against Bayern Munich as Dundee's greatest-ever team clinched it in the final three games of the campaign.

Symon's team improved further the following season and cruised to the championship despite having to play 12 games in eight weeks due to adverse weather conditions.

Celtic were convincingly beaten in the Scottish Cup final to hand Rangers a double. Ralph Brand grabbed two goals and Davie Wilson also netted as they inflicted a 3-0 drubbing on the Hoops in a replay.

Incredibly, the clean sweep of domestic trophies in season 1963/64 was a watershed for this fabulous Rangers side. It would be 11 years before they'd win another title and, to make matters worse, Celtic completed their historic nine-in-a-row during that time under manager Jock Stein.

In 1965 Baxter was controversially sold to Sunderland and, two years later, Symon was replaced by David White who endured an unsuccessful and perhaps luckless two-year spell at the club. He became the first boss in the history of the Govan club not to win a trophy, denied at the last by Bayern Munich in the 1967 Cup-Winners' Cup final.

Waddell was lured from Rugby Park to take over in 1969 in a bid to halt the club's slide and he would go on to have a bigger impact on Rangers as a manager than he did as a player.

The 1970/71 squad pose in that season's away strip

He was already a huge personality at the club by the time of the Ibrox Disaster in 1971. Waddell guided the club through one of the most difficult spells in its history when 66 people died in a crush on Stairway 13 after the New Year Old Firm derby against Celtic.

He was pictured, along with Parkhead boss Jock Stein, lifting the bodies of those who didn't survive off the Ibrox turf. Following the tragedy, Waddell vowed such an occurrence would never happen again and his vision of a safe, modern Ibrox is what you see today

Rangers fans mob John Greig after a famous victory

Colorsport

on match day. He put plans in place that would see the stadium become one of Europe's best.

A huge cloud was cast over the club in the aftermath of the tragedy and it was undoubtedly one of the lowest points in the club's history. Only a strong and inspirational figure could have led Rangers after the disaster and Waddell was perfect for that role. Amazingly, his side went on to lift a European trophy for the first time in 1972 with a memorable victory over Moscow Dynamo in the Nou Camp, Barcelona.

After defeating Stade Rennes, Sporting Lisbon, Torino and German giants Bayern Munich along the way, Willie Johnston's double and a Colin Stein strike sealed a memorable 3-2 victory over the Russians.

The win sparked wild celebrations and Rangers fans surged on to the field only to clash with over-zealous Spanish police. Sadly for skipper John Greig, he wasn't able to lift the trophy in public and was instead presented with the cup from UEFA officials in a room within the stadium.

But it was a fantastic achievement for Waddell and his men.

Almost immediately, he stood down from his role as manager and moved 'upstairs', as his coach Jock Wallace took over and set out to end Celtic's dominance on the domestic front.

KIT PARADE

Rangers Football Club and the colour 'royal blue' are synonymous with each other – the same way that red is with Liverpool or the green and white hoops of arch rivals Celtic are. It is the club's official colour and one which is recognised, along with the famous Rangers crest, by fans the world over.

The classic look of the shirt worn in the 1950s and 1960s

For almost the entirety of Rangers' existence the home shirt has been royal blue, with slight variations in colour and design over the years. The wide range of away kits and, recently, 'third' strips have changed more radically since the club was formed in 1872 but, by and large, have incorporated Rangers' other colours of red and white.

More recently, different shades of blue have been introduced, as well as a controversial 'tangerine' kit in 2002 which was a huge step away from tradition.

When Peter and Moses McNeill agreed with friends Peter Campbell and William McBeath to form a team called Rangers, after an English rugby club, the shirts worn by the team were described as 'light blue'. This was to distinguish them from the navy jerseys which were commonly worn by football teams around that time.

Rangers are regularly referred to as the 'light blues'. The nickname came about after the 1878 Scottish Cup final against Vale of Leven, when the team were described as the 'light and speedy blues'. This has been gradually shortened over the years.

For the first six years of Rangers' life, their unique kit consisted of the blue shirt with buttons at the right side of the neck, long white shorts and blue and white hooped socks. But in 1879/80, with Mr Angus Campbell as honorary secretary, a new kit was adopted – a blue and white hooped top, white shorts and hooped socks.

The crest appeared on the shirt for the first time in 1968

Later on, author John Allan wrote: "In 1879/80, the blue and white hoops were adopted. Matters had not been going too well with the team and Mr Campbell felt his responsibility. He was a true Highlander with a liberal strain of superstition in his being. A change of colours might change the luck so, at his suggestion, the old royal blue was packed away in the locker. Nobody was happy, however, until it was brought out again by a decree of a committee meeting in 1883. In royal blue, the Rangers have played ever since."

The only significant change to the club's kit in the next 26 years would be to the colour of the socks. They would range from navy blue to plain black before, in 1904, two red hoops were added to the turn-downs. This was the first introduction of red to the Rangers' home kit, a colour that would go on to become a prominent feature of the club's attire from then until the present day.

A sponsor's name appeared for the first time in 1984

In 1909 a white collar was brought in and, six years later, the sock turn-downs were changed to completely red – a look which was to become one of Rangers' great traditions.

Apart from slight variations to the collar and socks, the kit didn't alter too much in the next 53 years until in 1968 the famous RFC scroll crest was woven on to the home strip for the first time.

They also switched from a round collar to a v-neck – a few years after rivals Celtic had done the same.

Adidas introduced heavy branding to the kit design in 1992

In the period between Rangers' foundation and 1968, the club's away shirt changed far more frequently. Their first away strip was the iconic top worn between 1876 and 1879, which was plain white with a large blue star on the left breast.

Until 1934, the away kit mainly consisted of a white shirt with various different designs including a single blue hoop, or blue collar and cuffs. The shorts were mainly black, as were the socks with the red turn-downs.

Strangely, the RFC scroll badge appeared on the away jersey as early as 1918 and was used on and off between then and 1974. It has remained there permanently since.

From 1978, the Rangers home kit would be manufactured by Umbro for two decades and since then Admiral, Adidas, Nike and Diadora have all supplied kit for the club before a return to Umbro in 2005.

In that period, the shirt has had round neck, v-neck and flip collars, while also incorporating different features to adhere to the manufacturers' demands such as Adidas' three-stripes and the Nike tick.

The sock colour has also changed from plain blue to plain red to red with blue hoops. But in 1992 they returned to their traditional black with red-turn downs - a look which is now synonymous with the club.

Nike reintroduced a more muted design in 1997

In 1984, double-glazing firm CR Smith became Rangers' first shirt sponsor as they put their names to both Rangers and Celtic jerseys.

Since then, only McEwan's Lager, NTL and Carling have featured on the club's shirt – with brewers Tennent's appearing from the start of the 2010/11 season.

Away kits over the years have altered greatly but have rarely ventured away from the colours red and white. In 1994, the club introduced a specially-made shirt purely to be worn in European competition. It was a lilac strip with tiny air vents – supposedly to make it more comfortable playing abroad.

Two years later, taking

advantage of the club's global fan base and growing popularity, a 'third kit' was brought in which was red with white striped shoulders and had black shorts and socks. This idea is now common with most clubs in the UK and Gers' current third strip is all-white.

Navy and sky blue have been incorporated in the away kit at times but it was the 2002/03 orange kit which caused the most controversy. It was described as tangerine by the club and was supposed to be some sort of tribute to Rangers' Dutch manager Dick Advocaat. But many outsiders criticised the launch of the shirt with cynics accusing the club of cashing in on sectarianism and religious bigotry. It was ditched after just one season.

The most significant addition to the club's kit in the last decade came in 2003/04 when, after securing their 50th league championship the previous season, it was decided five stars would adorn the Rangers shirt – one for every 10 titles won in their illustrious history.

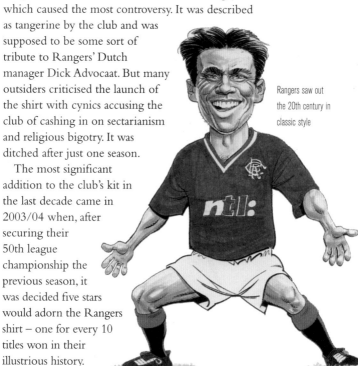

Rangers saw out the 20th century in classic style

HALL OF FAME

JIM BAXTER

If ever someone epitomised the phrase 'flawed genius' it would have to be midfield maestro Jim Baxter, arguably the most naturally-gifted footballer ever to pull on a Rangers jersey.

Born in Hill o'Beath on 29th September 1939, Baxter worked as a coal miner before joining Fife side Raith Rovers. He eventually joined Rangers for £17,500, a record fee in 1960, and became a true legend.

For five years he was a linchpin of Scot Symon's successful side and being the star of the show was second nature to the man affectionately known as 'Slim Jim'. The bigger the stage, the better he performed and he became a darling of the Ibrox crowd.

He had a magic wand for a left foot and his sublime skill and vision made him so easy on the eye. Baxter had a unique, almost languid style. He was arrogant and despite his Fife background he epitomised the Glasgow 'gallusness' that Rangers fans loved.

His swagger and ability to unlock opposition defences

with a single pass separated him from other midfielders in Scotland and he loved showcasing his skill against Rangers' and Scotland's fiercest rivals

> **ff He should have been Brazilian JJ**
> Pele

Baxter had an incredible record in Old Firm games. He played in 18 – ten League, five League Cup and three Scottish Cup – and lost just twice.

At international level, no Scotland fan will ever be able to forget the vision of him doing keepy-uppy at Wembley as the national side put England to the sword in 1967. Baxter masterminded the Scots' 3-2 victory against the then World Cup holders.

Tragically, he broke his leg in a European Cup tie against Rapid Vienna in 1964 – an injury which many felt cost the Ibrox men the trophy. After three months out, Slim Jim didn't return as the same player – and he was also becoming renowned for his off-field activities.

He was sold to Sunderland in May 1965 and moved on to Nottingham Forest before returning to Rangers four years later. It was an unsuccessful second stint and at the age of 31, Baxter hung up his boots for good.

Jim lost his fight with cancer in 2001 and football had lost one of the most colourful characters the game had ever seen.

Born: Hill o'Beath, 29th September 1929

Rangers appearances: 254

Rangers goals: 24

Honours won with Rangers: Scottish League (1961, 1963, 1964), Scottish Cup (1962, 1963, 1964), Scottish League Cup (1960, 1961, 1963, 1964)

Other clubs: Raith Rovers (1957), Sunderland (1965), Nottingham Forest (1967)

International appearances: Scotland, 34, 3 goals

JIM BAXTER FACTFILE

DAVIE COOPER

Most people say Davie Cooper's right leg was just for standing on. So it's just as well his left leg could do things with a football your average player can only dream about.

The image of 'Super Coop' – either in a Rangers or Scotland jersey – is ingrained in the history of the Scottish game.

Born in Hamilton in 1956, Cooper worked as an apprentice printer before his playing potential was picked out by Clydebank FC.

He was a key man in the club's charge towards the Second Division title, with a string of impressive performances attracting the attentions of the big clubs in England.

But Cooper craved a move to Rangers and, after a League Cup tie against the Ibrox side in 1976 when Cooper excelled, Gers' boss Jock Wallace paid £100,000 for his services.

Cooper was a traditional left winger but could also operate on the right – cutting in-field onto his magical left foot. In 12 years at Ibrox he would win three league titles, three Scottish Cups and an incredible seven League Cups. Also, Cooper scored what was voted the Greatest Ever Rangers Goal against Celtic at Hampden in the 1979 Drybrough Cup final.

ff He was one of the greatest players I'd ever seen JJ
Ruud Gullit

When Graeme Souness arrived at Rangers in 1986, Cooper was to play a huge part in his success at Ibrox. His cross at Pittodrie set up Terry Butcher to score the title-winning goal against Aberdeen – Gers' first championship success in nine years.

His goal against the Dons in the 1987 League Cup final will also go down in Ibrox folklore. A thunderous free-kick flew past Jim Leighton into the top corner, prompting one observer to remark "Leighton almost got a hand to it – on the way out!"

Cooper represented Scotland 24 times and played in the 1986 World Cup in Mexico under Alex Ferguson.

Coop eventually left Rangers in 1989 to sign for Motherwell and inspired them to Scottish Cup success in 1991.

He planned to finish his career at Clydebank but on 22nd March 1995 he collapsed after a brain haemorrhage.

He died the following day, aged just 39. Tributes poured in from around the globe as Ibrox mourned a legend.

Born: Hamilton, 25th February 1956

Rangers appearances: 540

Rangers goals: 75

Honours won with Rangers: Scottish League (1978, 1987, 1989), Scottish Cup (1978, 1979, 1981), Scottish League Cup (1978, 1979, 1981, 1982, 1984, 1985, 1987, 1988)

Other clubs: Clydebank (1974, 1994), Motherwell (1989)

International appearances: Scotland, 22, 6 goals

DAVIE COOPER FACTFILE

BARRY FERGUSON

One of the club's most successful captains of all time, Barry Ferguson deserves his place in the Ibrox Hall of Fame.

Born a Gers fan, and with a brother who also wore the light blue jersey, he dreamt of lifting trophies as a Rangers skipper. Incredibly, that dream was realised thanks to a Dutchman.

Dick Advocaat's arrival made Ferguson stay put after sporadic appearances under Walter Smith cast doubt over his first-team future. Advocaat made it clear he would build a team around the young playmaker and he was true to his word.

Ferguson was the linchpin of that successful new-look Gers team who won a domestic Treble in the Dutchman's first season in charge.

After winning another double in 2000, he was made captain but suffered a barren three-year spell without a trophy which resulted in Alex McLeish coming in as manager.

Gers lifted the League Cup and Scottish Cup that season as Ferguson got his hands on silverware for the first time as skipper. His stunning free kick in the 2002 Scottish Cup final at Hampden was the catalyst for a memorable victory over Celtic.

In McLeish's first full season, Ferguson was named Scotland's Player of the Year as he led the club to a Treble, but was snapped up by Blackburn Rovers for £7.5 million.

He failed to fully settle at Ewood Park and after just two seasons he made a sensational return to Ibrox. He was part of the 2005 title-winning side who clinched the championship in dramatic style against Hibs on the final day of the campaign.

Following Smith's return to Rangers in 2007, Ferguson became a key player in Gers' remarkable run to the UEFA Cup final in Manchester, where they lost to Zenit St Petersburg. Earlier that season, he had become Scotland's record holder for most appearances in Europe – eclipsing Kenny Dalglish.

In total, he won 15 major honours for Rangers but, after their title success in 2009, he was sold to Birmingham City and enjoyed a fantastic first season under his former gaffer McLeish in the Premiership.

> **ff He should be at Arsenal or Manchester United... he could play there too]]**
> Dick Advocaat

Born: Glasgow, 2nd February 1978

Rangers appearances: 289

Rangers goals: 44

Honours won with Rangers: Scottish League (1999, 2000, 2003, 2005, 2009), Scottish Cup (2000, 2002, 2003, 2008, 2009), Scottish League Cup (1998, 2002, 2003, 2005, 2008)

Other clubs: Blackburn Rovers (2003), Birmingham City (2009)

International appearances: Scotland, 22, 6 goals

BARRY FERGUSON FACTFILE

PAUL GASCOIGNE

Walter Smith pulled off a massive coup the day he persuaded Gazza to sign for Rangers. At one stage in his career, the England international was the most sought-after player in Europe.

The star of the 1990 World Cup in Italy, Gascoigne's maverick ability earned him a move to Lazio but injury had wrecked his time in Serie A. Even so, when Rangers registered an interest and paid £4.3 million for the midfielder in July 1995 it was one of the most sensational transfers in Scottish football history.

Off the pitch, Gascoigne was a loose cannon. On it, he was a genius and one of the most gifted players ever to pull on a blue jersey.

Inevitably, he became a fans' favourite at Ibrox almost instantly. In three seasons, he would cement his place in the hearts of Gers' supporters and take his place in the club's greatest-ever team.

In terms of quality, Gazza, along with Brian Laudrup, raised the bar at Rangers – often going on to win games single-handedly.

His strike rate was 39 goals in 103 games, a terrific

record for a central midfielder. Smith may have had his run-ins with him but he proved to be a world-class talent who was worth every penny Rangers paid.

In his first year at Ibrox, Smith's men would seal their eighth championship in a row, with Gascoigne at the heart of their title success.

Needing a win against Aberdeen to clinch it and a goal down, he took the game by the scruff of the neck and grabbed a memorable hat-trick. His second goal against the Dons was an incredible run from his own half, gliding past four players before finding the back of the net.

In 1997 he played a vital role in helping the club to a record-breaking nine-in-a-row – as well as producing a one-man show against Hearts in the League Cup final at Parkhead where his two goals effectively won it.

Gascoigned endured a troubled last season in Glasgow and, as the club chased yet another title, he was sold to Middlesbrough in March 1998 for £3.5 million.

Most Rangers fans believe if he'd stayed, they would have been celebrating ten-in-a-row.

> **" For any of us who have been lucky enough to be involved with him, he really was a phenomenal footballer "**
> Walter Smith

Born: Gateshead, 27th May 1967
Rangers appearances: 103
Rangers goals: 39
Honours won with Rangers:
Scottish League (1996, 1997), Scottish Cup (1996), Scottish League Cup (1996)
Other clubs: Newcastle United (1985), Tottenham Hotspur (1988), Lazio (1992), Middlesbrough (1998), Everton (2000), Burnley (2002), Gansu Tianma (2003), Boston United (2004)
International appearances: England, 57, 10 goals

PAUL GASCOIGNE FACTFILE

RICHARD GOUGH

He wasn't called 'Richard the Lionheart' for nothing. If anyone typified the spirit, desire, will to win and never say die attitude that was the cornerstone of Rangers' nine-in-a-row success under Walter Smith, captain Richard Gough was the man.

The defender was just one of three players to appear in every one of those record-breaking seasons, alongside Ally McCoist and Ian Ferguson. But only Gough collected all nine medals and that distinction makes him a unique Rangers skipper.

He'd have put his head through a brick wall for the club but the portrayal of him as a rugged centre back doesn't do him justice. Gough was a cultured footballer who could play from the back.

His main attributes were determination, passion and ability to deal with intense pressure. He started his career as a full back at Dundee United and later joined Tottenham Hotspur.

His performances at White Hart Lane prompted Graeme

Souness to spend £1.1 million to bring him to Ibrox in 1987.

His last-gasp equaliser against Celtic to earn a 2-2 draw in only his second game for the club made him an instant hero with the supporters and, from early on, Gough showed signs of being an inspirational defender. And when he took over the captaincy from Terry Butcher in 1990, his leadership qualities shone through.

As Rangers chased the holy grail of nine-in-a-row, he made it known he would leave the club in the summer of 1997 to play in America.

He was injured by the final day of the campaign when Brian Laudrup's goal sealed the championship against Dundee United and cemented that side's name in the history books.

In total Gough played 318 times for Rangers, winning 20 major honours. By October 1997, Smith brought him back to Ibrox for a second spell as they tried to seal an elusive tenth title on the trot.

It wasn't to be – even a colossus like Gough couldn't get them over the finishing line and his last game for Gers was the 1998 Scottish Cup final in which they suffered a 2-1 defeat to Hearts.

> **ff Looking back, Richard Gough was the best signing I ever made at Rangers JJ**
> Graeme Souness

RICHARD GOUGH FACTFILE

Born: Stockholm, 5th April 1962

Rangers appearances: 427

Rangers goals: 26

Honours won with Rangers: Scottish League (1987, 1989, 1990, 1991, 1992, 1993, 1994, 1995, 1996, 1997), Scottish Cup (1992, 1993, 1996), Scottish League Cup (1997)

Other clubs: Dundee United (1980), Tottenham Hotspur (1986), Kansas City Wizards (1997), San Jose Clash (1998), Everton (1999), Nottingham Forest (loan, 1999)

International appearances: Scotland, 61, 6 goals

ANDY GORAM

Andy Goram is known simply as 'The Goalie' around Ibrox and Scottish football. The mere mention of those two words evokes memories of Goram flying through the air and pulling off yet another sensational save.

He is Rangers' and Scotland's greatest ever goalkeeper and during the club's historic nine-in-a-row run, Goram looked unbeatable at times. So much so that former Celtic manager Tommy Burns was quoted as saying: "On my gravestone it will read Andy Goram broke my heart."

Despite his lack of height, he was a brilliant shot-stopper with terrific agility and lightening-quick reactions. When he did have to come for crosses he was strong in the punch and he didn't take any prisoners.

Goram was born in Bury and began his professional career with Oldham Athletic before joining Hibs in 1987, where his impressive form persuaded Walter Smith to splash out £1 million to bring him to Ibrox in 1991.

Despite a shaky start, Goram soon established himself as the undisputed number one. His best season at Ibrox was undoubtedly 1992/93 when Rangers embarked on a fantastic 44-game unbeaten run, lasting seven months in domestic and European competition. He played in every one of those games, conceding just 30 goals. His performances in both 'Battle of Britain' games against English champions Leeds United were outstanding. Gers would remain unbeaten in that competition as Goram and the team came within a whisker of reaching a European final.

ff When I pass away you can put it on my tombstone... Andy Goram broke my heart JJ
Tommy Burns

Invariably his best games for Rangers came in Old Firm games or crucial cup ties. Some of his displays against Burns' Celtic sides will go down in Ibrox folklore.

For Scotland, Goram won 43 caps and proved to be one of the world's best keepers at the 1996 European Championships in England.

When he finally left Ibrox in 1998, he went on to play for Motherwell and even enjoyed a brief spell at Manchester United under Sir Alex Ferguson. But Goram's heart will always be at Ibrox and it's unlikely anyone will ever take over the mantle of 'The Goalie'.

Born: Bury, 13th April 1964
Rangers appearances: 260
Rangers goals: 0
Honours won with Rangers:
Scottish League (1992, 1993, 1994, 1995, 1996, 1997), Scottish Cup (1992, 1993, 1996), Scottish League Cup (1992, 1993, 1996, 1998)
Other clubs: Oldham Athletic (1981, 2002), Hibernian (1987), Motherwell (1998), Sheffield United (1998), Notts County (1998), Manchester United (loan, 2001), Coventry City (2001), Hamilton Academicals (2001), Queen of the South (2002), Coventry City, Elgin City (2003)
International appearances: Scotland, 43

ANDY GORAM FACTFILE

JOHN GREIG

'Greatest Ever Ranger'. That's how John Greig will be forever remembered at Ibrox. As a player, he amassed 753 appearances, in the process winning five league championships, six Scottish Cups, four League Cups and 44 Scotland caps.

As the club's manager, he won another two Scottish Cups and two League Cups.

In short, John Greig is Mr Rangers. In an association which has now lasted 49 years, Greig has seen it all at Ibrox, from a tragic disaster to lifting a European trophy, from title success to dismal failure. Greig is the embodiment of Rangers.

During his 18 years as a player he was an inspirational captain who got his hands on the club's solitary piece of European silverware in 1972 when Rangers secured victory over Moscow Dynamo in the Cup-Winners' Cup final at the Nou Camp, Barcelona.

He was a versatile player who was equally as effective at full back, wing half or inside forward. Left sided, Greig could defend like a lion but also loved to venture forward down the flank.

Ask any Rangers supporter about John Greig and the words passion, spirit and desire will roll off the tongue.

As captain of Scotland, several English clubs were keen on signing Greig at his peak. But he stayed with Rangers.

That loyalty and strength of character made him a legendary figure in the eyes and hearts of the Ibrox faithful. He had an incredible will to win and never-say-die attitude which earned him enormous respect from his fellow players, managers and supporters.

It wasn't all plain sailing, though, for Greig. He had to endure Celtic's nine-in-a-row glory years and the torture of watching Gers' great rivals win the European Cup.

But he saw it through and emerged to go and achieve huge success as a player. As a manager, he found it tough replacing Jock Wallace in 1978.

Despite winning four cups, his team couldn't get their hands on the league title and Greig resigned in October 1983.

Greig, who received an MBE for his services to football, has been one of the most influential men in the history of the club and in 2003 was made a director.

> **" You always wanted to be in any team that John Greig was in "**
> Derek Johnstone

JOHN GREIG FACTFILE

Born: Edinburgh, 11th September 1942

Rangers appearances: 755

Rangers goals: 120

Honours won with Rangers:
Scottish Premier League (1963, 1964, 1975 1976, 1978),
Scottish Cup (1962, 1963, 1964, 1966, 1973, 1976, 1978),
Scottish League Cup (1964, 1965, 1976, 1978), European Cup Winners' Cup (1972)

Other clubs: None

International appearances: Scotland, 44, 3 goals

BRIAN LAUDRUP

It's rare for a footballer to have a match named after him. But to everyone who was at Hampden on 18th May 1996, the Scottish Cup final will always be remembered as The Laudrup Final.

Brian Laudrup was no ordinary footballer. The fact that Gordon Durie scored a hat-trick that day against Hearts in Rangers' stunning 5-1 victory tells you everything about the Danish winger's performance.

He produced a breathtaking display to rip the Jambos apart, scoring twice and creating three for Durie to ensure Gers secured another domestic double.

Laudrup's signing at Ibrox in July 1994 was a coup for boss Walter Smith, who managed to tempt him to Glasgow from Fiorentina for £2.3 million. He would prove to be one of the best buys Smith ever made.

He'd begun his career at Brondby before signing for German side Uerdingen and then Bundesliga giants Bayern Munich. As his reputation around Europe grew, Laudrup played his part in Denmark's success at the 1992 European Championships when they defied the odds to lift the trophy.

After a disappointing spell in Italy, Laudrup re-invented himself in Scotland and Rangers reaped the benefits. He became an instant hit with the Ibrox support who were mesmerised by his sublime skill and electrifying acceleration with the ball at his feet.

Since the days of Willie Henderson, Jim Baxter and then Davie Cooper, the supporters had never witnessed anyone as exciting as Laudrup and defences simply couldn't cope with him. At times, he was destroying teams on his own – either scoring himself or laying chances on a plate for others.

He hit ten goals in his first season, helping Rangers clinch seven-in-a-row and picked up both Player of the Year awards for his exceptional wing play.

The following year he was joined at Gers by Paul Gascoigne, giving the club two genuine world-class performers at their disposal.

After securing the eighth consecutive title, Laudrup sealed the record-equalling ninth when he headed the winning goal at Tannadice in 1997.

It's no wonder Gers fans used to sing 'There's only one Brian Laudrup'.

ff Other than getting a couple of blokes to beat him up, I have no idea how to cope with Brian Laudrup JJ

Jim Duffy (ex-Dundee manager)

Born: Vienna, 22nd February 1969

Rangers appearances: 150

Rangers goals: 45

Honours won with Rangers: Scottish League (1995, 1996, 1997), Scottish Cup (1996), Scottish League Cup (1997)

Other clubs: Brondby (1986), Bayer Uerdingen (1989), Bayern Munich (1990), Fiorentina (1992), AC Milan (loan, 1993), Chelsea (1998), FC Copenhagen (1999), Ajax (1999)

International appearances: Denmark, 75, 21 goals

BRIAN LAUDRUP FACTFILE

ALLY MCCOIST

Rangers have been blessed with some phenomenal strikers but Ally McCoist is, quite simply, the greatest of them all. And few players have been as popular at Ibrox as 'Super Ally'.

The club's leading post-war goalscorer made the number nine shirt his own in 15 glorious years, during which time he won two European Golden Boots. It's unlikely McCoist's achievements will ever be surpassed.

He started his career with St Johnstone, where he was first deployed as a midfielder. He was eventually moved up front and won a move to Sunderland in 1981, where he struggled to find the net.

John Greig signed him for Rangers in 1983 and he was part of a poor side. It's almost unthinkable to imagine McCoist as anything other than a hero among the supporters, but it took him time to win them over.

When he did, he went on to become a true Gers legend. He scored an incredible 251 goals, which included 28 hat-tricks and a total of 27 goals against Old Firm rivals Celtic.

He flourished in the early Graeme Souness era but, following the signing of Mark Hateley, McCoist was relegated to the bench. It's testament to his character that he knuckled down to become a mainstay under Walter Smith during the historic nine-in-a-row years – with Hateley as his strike partner.

His last match for Rangers was the 1998 Scottish Cup final but it was to be no fairytale ending. Despite scoring, Rangers lost 2-1 to Hearts and Smith's all-conquering side was immediately dismantled by Dick Advocaat.

Having scored 19 goals for Scotland and featured at the 1990 World Cup, he became assistant manager of the national side alongside his old gaffer Smith in 2004.

But McCoist was always destined for a return to Rangers and became Smith's right-hand man at Ibrox in January 2007. He has helped the club lift two SPL titles and reach the 2008 UEFA Cup final.

It would be fitting if, as expected, McCoist replaces Smith one day and becomes manager of the club he loves.

> **Coisty scored 335 goals in 581 games for the club and is – as he keeps telling me – Rangers' greatest ever striker**
>
> Barry Ferguson

Born: Bellshill, 24th September 1962

Rangers appearances: 581

Rangers goals: 355

Honours won with Rangers:
Scottish League (1987, 1989, 1990, 1991, 1992, 1993, 1994, 1995, 1996, 1997), Scottish Cup (1992), Scottish League Cup (1983, 1984, 1986, 1987, 1988, 1990, 1992, 1993, 1996)

Other clubs: St Johnstone (1979), Sunderland (1981), Kilmarnock (1998)

International appearances: Scotland, 61, 19 goals

ALLY MCCOIST FACTFILE

ALAN MORTON

The man nicknamed 'The Wee Blue Devil' used to torment defenders in the days in which he wore a Rangers shirt.

Despite being followed by the likes of Willie Henderson, Davie Wilson, Davie Cooper and Brian Laudrup, many believe Morton to be the club's greatest ever winger. There's a portrait of him at the top of the Ibrox main stand's famous marble staircase and that indicates just how much the memory of Morton is still treasured within the club.

He was legendary boss Bill Struth's first signing for Rangers in 1920 from Queen's Park and it proved to be an astute one. He was just 5ft 4ins tall but the Jordanhill-born wide man didn't let his lack of height affect his performances.

In fact, Morton would go on to be one of the most exciting and entertaining players in the club's history. He was part of the Gers' side who hammered rivals Celtic 4-0 in the 1928 Scottish Cup final, a victory which ended a 25-year wait to lift the trophy. In his 13 years at Ibrox he won an astonishing ten league championships, as well as two Scottish Cups. In

495 matches for the club he scored 115 goals, as well as many assists, and was an integral part of Struth's all-conquering side.

He used his speed, balance, close control and terrific ball skills to bamboozle opposition defenders as he provided a constant supply line to Rangers' strikers at that time, who gratefully finished off his good work.

His nickname was "The Wee Society Man", no doubt stemming from his immaculate appearance. Morton would walk into Ibrox each day for training dressed in a suit, wearing gloves and a bowler hat. He personified Rangers' image off the field and on it.

Morton was also a superb servant to Scotland and will always be remembered as one of the 'Wembley Wizards'. In 1928 at the home of the Auld Enemy, the Rangers winger helped destroy England 5-1 and his display in London earned him his moniker 'The Wee Blue Devil'. And no wonder, as three of his crosses that day were converted by team-mate Alex Jackson.

He played 11 times against the English in his 31-cap career and Morton is regarded as not only a Rangers great, but a Scotland legend too.

> ❝ **There's never been one to equal him. He would have been acclaimed today as he was acclaimed in his day... as the Supremo** ❞
>
> William Allison (former Rangers historian)

ALAN MORTON FACTFILE

Born: Jordanhill, 24th April 1893

Rangers appearances: 495

Rangers goals: 115

Honours won with Rangers: Scottish League (1921, 1923, 1924, 1925, 1927, 1928, 1929, 1930, 1931), Scottish Cup (1928, 1930)

Other clubs: Queen's Park

International appearances: Scotland, 31, 5 goals

HELICOPTER SUNDAY

'Keep believing' was the Rangers motto towards the end of the 2004/05 SPL season. Devout Christian and Ibrox centre back Marvin Andrews coined the phrase and it struck a chord with the Ibrox fans.

If Alex McLeish's side were to go on to win the championship in miraculous style, they had to keep believing. On 22nd May 2005 at Easter Road, their faith was rewarded.

That day in Edinburgh, now known as Helicopter Sunday, will go down as one of the most dramatic in the club's 138-year history. It has recently been voted by supporters as Rangers' Game of the Decade and for anyone who was there, the unforgettable 90 minutes is etched in the memory.

McLeish's team had won the SPL title two years previously on the last day of the 2003 campaign. A nerve-shredding afternoon at Ibrox had ended in a 6-1 victory over Dunfermline, pipping Celtic to the title on goal difference. Helicopter Sunday eclipsed even that day's drama.

There had been little between Rangers and Celtic at the start of the season, as Martin O'Neill's side set

out to retain their SPL crown and heap pressure on
McLeish who, unlike previous Gers managers, was
working within a tight budget.

Rangers had capitulated in the 2003/04 season and
no one expected the Ibrox club to run Celtic so close
the following year. Celtic won the first Old Firm derby
but Rangers gained revenge
in the corresponding home
fixture, as well as beating the
Hoops 2-1 in the League Cup.

By early in January the Ibrox
men had been knocked out
of the UEFA Cup and the
Scottish Cup – by Celtic –
but clinched the League Cup
at Hampden with a thumping
5-1 victory over Motherwell.

Between March and
May, it was a straight fight
between the Glasgow giants
for the championship. But
Celtic had pulled a rabbit out of a hat in the transfer
window by enticing Craig Bellamy to Parkhead on loan.

Nacho Novo is
hoisted high by
Fernando Ricksen
as Rangers
celebrate…

The Premiership star made an immediate impact and
when his goal at Ibrox helped O'Neill's men to a 2-1 win
over Rangers on 24th April, the title looked destined for
Celtic Park.

With four games left, McLeish's side trailed by five
points and it seemed impossible to bring the trophy
back to Govan. The Rangers manager said: "It's difficult

to see Celtic losing it now. They can only throw it away but we'll keep going and hope for a slip-up."

His own side kept their side of the bargain by winning their next three matches. And Celtic's shock 3-1 loss at the hands of Hibs gave Rangers hope.

It would all come down to the final game of the season, with Gers visiting Easter Road and Celts travelling to Fir Park to face Motherwell. The Hoops were two points clear so Rangers had to beat Hibs – a tough ask in itself – and hope for a miracle in Lanarkshire.

With half an hour gone Rangers' forlorn hopes had already been shattered by Chris Sutton's goal which put Celtic one-up against a Well side with nothing left to play for.

McLeish's side had to battle against a Hibees outfit who were fighting for a UEFA Cup spot. Nacho Novo's goal on 59 minutes put them in the driving seat and, bizarrely, the 1-0 scoreline suited both sides as it would give Rangers the win they needed and allow Hibs into Europe on goal difference.

It was simply a case of waiting, and praying, for a Motherwell goal at Fir Park.

With 88 minutes on the clock, some Gers fans left the stadium, reluctantly conceding defeat to their bitter rivals. But incredibly Motherwell, managed by Rangers legend Terry Butcher, made it 1-1. The roar from the Rangers end which greeted news of Scott McDonald's goal almost took the roof off Easter Road's South Stand.

All of a sudden, after 38 gruelling matches, McLeish's

men were within two minutes of the league flag.

A helicopter, with the SPL trophy on board, had been preparing to go to Fir Park but as one radio commentator famously bellowed, "the helicopter is changing direction".

The Rangers supporters couldn't believe what was happening – and neither could the players on the pitch, who were frantically trying to get word from the bench about events at Fir Park.

It was surreal. But when McDonald scored a sensational second goal in injury time, it was all over. While Celtic fans wept, the Gers support went wild in celebration.

The full time whistle hadn't gone yet at Easter Road but the players began punching the air as they realised they were champions. At time up, there were scenes of joy in the stands and on the pitch as Rangers clinched their 51st championship in the most amazing fashion.

... leaving Celtic fans in despair and disbelief at what had happened

They had to wait for the helicopter to re-route to Edinburgh but it was all worth it as skipper Fernando Ricksen lifted the trophy in front of a jubilant away support.

Cult figure Andrews, who had urged the Rangers fans to 'keep believing', had got it spot on.

THE RANGERS STORY
MAKING HISTORY
1972-98

The Barcelona Bears had instantly become Rangers legends after their European triumph and for the rest of the 1970s they also enjoyed a fair measure of success on the domestic scene.

In Jock Wallace's first year in charge, 1972/73, his team lifted the Scottish Cup after a thrilling 3-2 win over Celtic at Hampden with Tam Forsyth scoring a memorable 'tap-in' to clinch the trophy. But real success was achieved three years later when Celtic's stranglehold on the title was broken. Colin Stein's goal at Easter Road in a 1-1 draw with Hibs crushed The Hoops' hopes of ten-in-a-row.

The new ten-team Scottish Premier League was introduced the next year and Rangers would be the first champions.

It was a historic year for Wallace and the Ibrox men as a tense win over Celtic in the League Cup final was followed up by a comprehensive 3-1 defeat of Hearts in the Scottish Cup final at Hampden.

With John Greig still leading from the front as captain, the light blues had secured the domestic treble for only the third time in the club's history.

After a barren season, the same trio of silverware would be back in the Ibrox trophy room in 1978. Aberdeen were pipped to the title and Scottish Cup final, while Celtic were disposed of in the League Cup final.

But despite being the first Rangers manager to win two trebles Wallace quit abruptly, many believe after a disagreement with Willie Waddell and the Rangers board although that has never been confirmed.

European Cup-Winners' Cup captain Greig was Waddell's number one choice to take over and he wasted no time in offering the Edinburgh-born player the job. Greig became Rangers' seventh boss on 24th May 1978.

In his first campaign Greig's team lifted both cups, but the championship was lost to Celtic after a 4–2 loss at Parkhead near the end of the season. A point would have most probably kept the championship in Govan.

The 1978/79 squad pose with the treble trophies won in the previous campaign

Some say Greig never recovered from that, but
other factors also conspired against him. It wasn't
easy for the Rangers stalwart to break up a team of
legends who were coming to the end of their careers.
And Aberdeen and Dundee United were enjoying
the best periods in their history both in Scotland
and in Europe.

Robert Prytz takes
on the rain and Celtic
in a 1982 derby

In 1979/80 Rangers finished a poor fifth in the
league and failed to qualify for Europe. And a Scottish
Cup final appearance ended in turmoil. After Celtic
had won the game 1-0 in extra time, fans of both
clubs invaded the pitch and rioted before mounted
police were able to seize control. Many people were
injured and the upshot was alcohol being banned
from all football grounds across the country.

Rangers had become a decent cup
team unable to find consistency in the
league. The pressure took its toll on
Greig, who eventually resigned on 28th
October 1983.

Both Alex Ferguson at Pittodrie and
Jim McLean at Tannadice turned the
Ibrox job down, so Wallace returned to
the club for a second spell in charge.
Sadly for the light blue hordes who
adored the man from Wallyford, it was far
less productive than his first.

He won two League Cups but the
team couldn't break into the Premier
League's top three. In 1985/86, they
slumped to fifth again with just 35 points
from 36 games, a low point in the club's
history. Wallace couldn't survive.

His replacement, announced before the
end of the season, sent shockwaves right
through the Scottish game. Graeme
Souness was to be player-manager and the

former Scotland, Liverpool and Sampdoria midfielder transformed the club on and off the park.

Souness was given big money to spend in the transfer market and signed top English stars like Chris Woods, Terry Butcher, Gary Stevens, Ray Wilkins, Trevor Steven and Mark Hateley over the following years.

After a controversial start – he was sent off in the opening game of the season at Hibs for a bad challenge on former Celtic striker George McCluskey – he led Rangers to the title, with a Butcher header in a 1-1 draw against Aberdeen at Pittodrie sparking wild celebrations. The League Cup had been won earlier in the season with a 2-1 win over Celtic but as the rebuilding job continued, a disappointing season followed. It was in season 1988/89 that the Souness Revolution really kicked in as Gers won the first of a historic nine titles in a row.

David Murray had taken over as owner of the club and, over time, £90 million was spent on players, with £52 million splashed out on redeveloping Ibrox Stadium.

Souness and Murray were also responsible for Rangers signing their first high-profile Roman Catholic in decades when ex-Celtic striker Mo Johnstone arrived from Nantes to smash down any religious barriers which remained.

But with Rangers on course for their third successive title win, Souness controversially left to become Liverpool manager – a decision he later regretted.

His assistant Walter Smith took over and would go on to become one of the most successful bosses in Rangers' history, able to stand alongside the likes of Struth, Symon and Waddell before him.

Mark Hateley was one of the English stars brought to Rangers by Graeme Souness

During the 1992/93 campaign, Rangers came within a whisker of making it to the Champions League final but were pipped by eventual winners Marseille. The same season saw Gers embark on a remarkable 44-game unbeaten run to secure their fifth championship on the spin.

Smith began to attract players like Brian Laudrup and Paul Gascoigne to Ibrox but their European achievements of 1993 couldn't be matched. On the domestic front, though, the Holy Grail of nine-in-a-row was in their sights.

Ally and Gazza are all smiles after the 1996 Coca Cola Cup victory

It was finally clinched at Tannadice on 7th May 1997 against Dundee United when a Laudrup header sealed a 1-0 win. Smith and his team had

equalled Celtic's record to carve their names into Rangers' folklore.

The question was, could they beat it and make it ten? Sadly, they fell just short and, after Gascoigne's departure and Smith's revelation that he'd stand down at the end of the campaign, momentum was lost and Wim Jansen's Celtic took the title.

It was the end of an era for a legendary Rangers team and legends such as Andy Goram, Richard Gough and Ally McCoist left the club after an agonising Scottish Cup final defeat to Hearts at Parkhead.

Smith also departed but owner Murray wouldn't let the club stand still as he appointed Rangers' first-ever foreign boss.

Fans' smiles were even broader in 1997 as the club secured nine-in-a-row

RANGERS

COMIC STRIP HISTORY

3

WHILST IN CHARGE OF A GAME BETWEEN RANGERS AND HIBS, THE REFEREE DROPPED HIS YELLOW CARD. WHEN PLAY STOPPED, PAUL GASCOIGNE PICKED IT UP AND 'GAVE' IT BACK TO HIM...

I'M GOING TO HAVE TO BOOK YOU, REF...

THE REF DIDN'T SEE THE FUNNY SIDE, INSTEAD...

YOU ARE THE ONE WHO IS BOOKED, GASCOIGNE... FOR YOUR CHEEK!

AW, COME ON, REF...

HE WAS ONLY HAVING A BIT OF FUN...

GAZZA HAD THE LAST LAUGH. HE WENT ON TO SCORE THE SPL'S GOAL OF THE SEASON, AS RANGERS ROMPED TO A 7-0 WIN!

TACTICS

JOCK WALLACE: FITNESS FIRST

Jock Wallace took over a Rangers team that had just lifted the Cup-Winner's Cup . Their 1972 success in Barcelona is the only piece of European silverware to the club's name. But on the domestic front, they were lagging behind rivals Celtic.

Wallace was more of a tactician than people perceived and he moulded his team to suit the way he wanted his side to play. Jock Stein's Celtic were on their way to winning nine championships on the trot. Their monopoly of the Scottish game simply gave Wallace more motivation to break that stranglehold and bring the title back to Ibrox.

He laid down a marker in his first season by defeating the Hoops in the 1973 Centenary Scottish Cup thanks to Tam Forsyth's winning goal at Hampden Park. But it took him another two years to rebuild Gers and make them champions again.

In 1975 Colin Stein, one of the Barcelona Bears who had returned to the club after a spell at Coventry, scored the goal in a 1-1 draw at Hibs which sealed the title and prevented Celtic from making it ten-in-a-row.

The signings of Davie Cooper and Bobby Russell were key. Wallace liked big, tall strikers like Derek Johnstone, Derek Parlane and Martin Henderson but he also knew how important the service to his front men was and that's where the likes of Cooper and Tommy McLean excelled, patrolling the flanks in what was essentially a 4-2-4 formation.

Above all, Wallace knew his team had to be fitter than anyone else in the Scottish League. His training stints at Gullane Sands are legendary even now and the pictures of exhausted Gers stars trying to climb 'Murder Hill' are now part of Scottish football folklore.

The combination of tactical awareness and masterful motivation helped make Wallace the only Rangers boss to win two domestic trebles.

GRAEME SOUNESS: HARD MEN WHO COULD PLAY

Rangers needed a lift when Graeme Souness stunned the football world by announcing he was taking over as player-manager at Ibrox. The former Liverpool and Scotland star was enticed into the role by chairman David Holmes and charged with the task of bringing Rangers back to life.

He achieved that and more, revolutionising Scottish football in the process. Holmes's appointment of Walter Smith as the inexperienced Souness's assistant was a masterstroke.

But it was Souness's strategy in the transfer market which transformed the Scottish game and lifted Gers out of the doldrums. His sole aim in 1986 was simple – to win back the Premier League title. He had a small group of talented Scots like Ian Durrant, Ally McCoist, Derek Ferguson and Davie Cooper, who were ready to excel. But he needed a spine, a solid core of experience. And he knew exactly where to find them.

Souness scoured England and lured international goalkeeper Chris Woods to Ibrox. But his spectacular signing of then England captain Terry Butcher was a signal of intent. Over time, a host of English stars made the trip to Glasgow, as did Scotland skipper Richard Gough who arrived from Spurs. He would captain Rangers to nine league titles in a row.

Souness had bought the club a backbone. It wasn't about tactics, this was a fairly orthodox, solid 4-4-2, it was about players with leadership, hunger, desire and quality – traits he had himself in abundance.

Fittingly, it was skipper Butcher who headed home the goal that sealed the championship at Pittodrie in 1987 against Aberdeen.

Souness had needed hard men who could play in order to bring success to Ibrox. No one can say he didn't deliver.

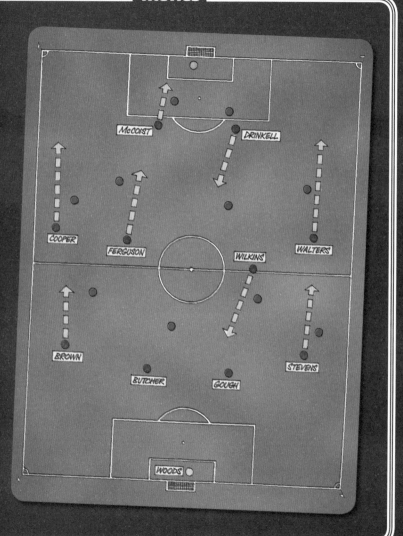

DICK ADVOCAAT: TOTAL FOOTBALL

Dick Advocaat was appointed as Rangers' first foreign manager in 1998 and brought with him a brand of football which hadn't been seen at Ibrox in years. He had been brought up as a disciple of Dutch Total Football and chairman David Murray believed Advocaat's methods could help the club lift a European trophy for the first time in almost 30 years.

The signings of Dutch stars Arthur Numan, Michael Mols and Giovanni van Bronckhorst were crucial, as was the promotion of Ibrox youngster Barry Ferguson. The likes of Claudio Reyna, Rod Wallace and Neil McCann were also vital acquisitions.

Gers' entire midfield were all creative and comfortable on the ball. Having a classy goalscoring midfielder in the shape of Dutch international Ronald De Boer did no harm either. Up front, Mols and Wallace struck up a productive partnership, with the Englishman dropping off the front to link up his midfield and creating space for the wide men to push on to devastating effect. Mols could also operate across the front line as a lone striker, with De Boer sitting in behind and Reyna a third option from deep.

The beauty of Advocaat, though, was his ability to surprise. Against PSV Eindhoven in 1999/00 he drafted in fringe star Derek McInnes from nowhere and asked him to man-mark danger man Luc Nilis. It worked a treat as Gers recorded a 4-1 Ibrox win over the Dutch champions.

The following season against Monaco, Turkish midfielder Tugay was deployed in a sweeper role and again Advocaat got his tactics spot on as Rangers emerged from France with a priceless 1-0 victory.

He may not have realised Murray's long-term vision but, most fans would agree the Dutchman's tactics served up some of the best football ever witnessed at Ibrox.

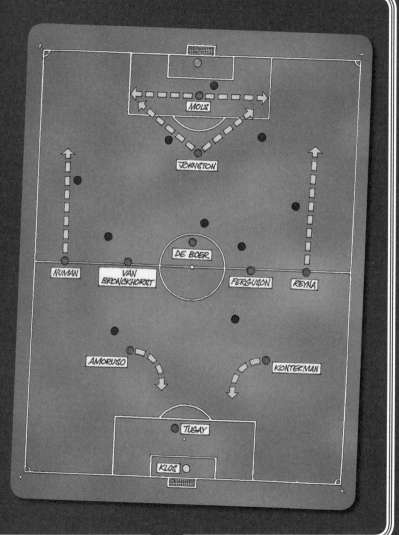

WALTER SMITH: ANTI-FOOTBALL?

Lionel Messi called it 'anti-football'. But the Barcelona star can't say Walter Smith's tactics in getting Rangers to a European final weren't successful.

When Smith had returned to Ibrox in 2007 it was a different club to the one he'd left behind in 1998, with finances severely limited. He could only work with the tools at his disposal and, as Gers embarked on an epic European journey, Smith's 4-2-3-1 system paid off in spectacular fashion as he took them all the way to the UEFA Cup final.

The Euro adventure started in the Champions League. His defensive formation wasn't pretty but it was effective and teams found Rangers difficult to break down. Carlos Cuellar and David Weir provided the base at the back. In front of them, sitting midfielders Brahim Hemdani and Christian Dailly were insurance, with Barry Ferguson as the playmaker. Steven Davis and Charlie Adam were deployed in wide areas. Either Jean-Claude Darcheville or Daniel Cousin operated as the lone front man and both played their part in a memorable run to the final in Manchester where Gers eventually lost to Russian side Zenit St Petersburg.

Along the way, there was a 3-0 away win in Lyon, a 3-2 victory over Stuttgart at Ibrox and that goalless draw against Barcelona which prompted Messi's anti-football jibe.

After dropping into the UEFA Cup, Gers secured brilliant results against Panathanaikos, Werder Bremen, Sporting Lisbon and Fiorentina.

Their success was built on resilience, strength and determination but in Lisbon, for example, Smith's men also played some fantastic counter-attacking football to beat the Portuguese side 2-0. In Messi's eyes it was anti-football. In Smith's and the Rangers fans' eyes it was winning football.

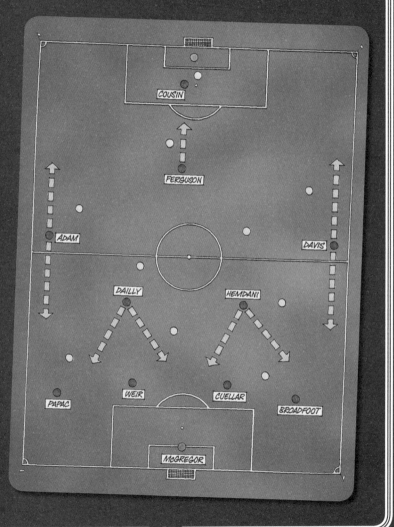

GREAT
GAFFERS

The standards set by Bill Struth at Ibrox helped shape the club into what it is today. An imposing figure, he laid down the foundations for others to build on and installed traditions and values which those who would follow had to adhere to.

It's fitting that the stadium's main stand is named after Struth as his influence and impact on Rangers should never be forgotten. That's why his portrait still hangs in the famous trophy room – a symbol of his importance in the club's history. He coined the phrase which has become a mantra of the club – "Let the others come after us, we welcome the chase."

When William Wilton tragically drowned in a 1920 boating accident, Struth became only the club's second manager. At 45 years old, no one could possibly have predicted the period of unrivalled success he would embark on over the next three decades.

His record at Ibrox is extraordinary and unsurpassed. Struth won the Scottish League Championship 18 times, which

The legendary Bill Struth, pictured here tending his tomatoes

included an incredible run of 14 titles in 19 years before the Second World War. He's the man who won Rangers their first domestic double in 1928, then their first treble in 1949.

Struth had players at his disposal who would go on
to become greats at the club like Alan Morton, Bob
McPhail, Willie Thornton, Willie Woodburn and
George Young. But it was his strong man-management
and strict discipline which truly made him a force to
be reckoned with inside Ibrox. He made sure his
players knew it was special to wear the light blue shirt
and if anyone fell below the standards he demanded,
their feet wouldn't touch the ground.

Struth became a director in 1947 and was
appointed vice-chairman when he
retired as manager in summer 1954.
He died two years later, aged 81.

Scot Symon would replace Struth
and continued to live up to the
traditions Rangers were now known
by. His time at the club ended in
1967 and after David White's
two-year spell at the helm, Willie
Waddell took over as manager.

For almost half a century he
would contribute more to Rangers
than any other man in their history.
As a player, manager and executive at
Ibrox, he is now a legendary figure
who is credited with lifting the club
from its knees.

He had been a phenomenal winger under Struth
years previously but by the time he returned as boss,
there was a cloud hanging over Gers. Waddell, with his

Willie Waddell served
the club for almost
half a century

Jock Wallace took over the reins from his former boss Waddell

unwavering single-mindedness and long-term vision, set out with desire and determination to place Rangers at the top of the pile again.

He had already guided Kilmarnock to their only ever championship success in 1965 and after a stint as a journalist he was appointed Rangers manager in December 1969. He led them to their first trophy success since 1966 when they lifted the 1970 League Cup with a victory over Celtic at Hampden. But the task of bringing former glories back to Govan was made even more difficult following the Ibrox Disaster of 1971, in which 66 people lost their lives in a stairway crush following an Old Firm derby.

The tragedy tested the resolve of Waddell but he thrived on the challenge and showed tremendous leadership qualities. He insisted on players and staff attending every one of the funerals and thereafter set about re-developing Ibrox. Today's UEFA five-star stadium is a result of Waddell's vision and it was he who initiated its new-look structure.

While doing that, he somehow led the club to its first and only European trophy to date. Just a year after the Ibrox tragedy, captain John Greig lifted the 1972 European Cup-Winners' Cup in Barcelona after Rangers beat Moscow Dynamo 3-2 in the final.

After that triumph, Waddell handed the reins to coach Jock Wallace. When Waddell died in 1992, he was remembered as a man who had given his life to Rangers and he left behind a huge legacy which is now revered around the world.

Jock Wallace enjoyed unprecedented success in his first six-year spell as Rangers manager, leading them to their two glorious trebles in the space of just three years. Wallace had been drafted in as Waddell's right-hand man in 1970.

Wallace's training methods are now legendary and still send a shiver down the spine of some former Gers stars. He was a hard taskmaster, a fitness fanatic who fought as a commando in the jungles of Malaysia. The players regularly found themselves running up and down the sand dunes of Gullane as part of their pre-season routine, but the hard work paid off.

In 1974/75 Wallace led Gers to

Graeme Souness revolutionised not just the club, but the whole of Scottish football

championship success for the first time in 11 years. The following year, his side scooped a league, Scottish Cup and League Cup treble – a feat which they repeated in 1977/78.

Wallace struck fear into his players and set about fostering a team spirit which couldn't be matched by any other team in Scotland at that time.

Despite winning that 'double treble' he shocked fans by resigning after what was rumoured to be a dispute with Waddell and the Ibrox board. He took over at Leicester City but would eventually return to Rangers in 1983.

He may not have enjoyed the same success second time around but Wallace will always be remembered as a great leader of the club.

John Greig couldn't emulate what he'd done as a player at Rangers in the dugout when he became boss in 1978. After failing to win the championship he departed and Wallace returned for his ill-fated second stint at Ibrox.

Walter Smith celebrates the 1991 league title with his players

By 1986 the club needed re-awakening and Graeme Souness did that as player-manager. He enticed the cream of English football to sign for Rangers and revolutionised the whole of Scottish football. But after five years at the club, he stunned supporters by leaving for Liverpool and was replaced by a man who would go on to become a modern-day Rangers legend.

After a modest career as a player at Dumbarton and Dundee United, Walter Smith became a coach at Tannadice under legendary gaffer Jim McLean. In 1986, Gers chairman David Holmes threw Souness and Smith together at Rangers and it was a dream partnership. Smith became the club's tenth manager when Souness departed for Anfield.

Smith has become one of the iconic Rangers managers

He will be forever remembered as the man who led the club to a record-breaking nine titles in a row, equalling Celtic's feat of the 1960s. But after missing out on a tenth successive championship in 1998, Smith resigned and was replaced by Dutch coach Dick Advocaat.

He was followed by Alex McLeish and Paul Le Guen before answering an SOS call in 2007 to return to the club he loved. In 2008, Rangers reached the UEFA Cup final but lost 2-0 to Zenit St Petersburg in the final in Manchester.

In the last three years, Smith has led Rangers to six trophies and now stands alongside Ibrox's iconic managerial figures, Struth, Waddell and Wallace.

MEMORABLE
MATCHES

RANGERS 3
MOSCOW DYNAMO 2

European Cup-Winners' Cup final, Camp Nou
Stadium, 24th May 1972

The 'Barcelona Bears' will have their names ingrained in
Rangers' history forever. To this day, those 11 players
are the select band who have got their hands on a
European trophy for the Ibrox club.

Their 3-2 win over Moscow Dynamo in the Nou
Camp Stadium will never be forgotten and that's why
the team who lifted the Cup-Winner's Cup will always
be revered by the Gers' faithful.

Boss Willie Waddell had the unenviable task of
leading the club following the Ibrox disaster in January
1971, when 66 people died at the
end of the game during a crush
on stairway 13. Their league
campaign suffered badly as they
tried to recover from the tragic
loss but in Europe the Light
Blues thrived. Rennes and
Sporting Lisbon were beaten in
the opening rounds followed by
Torino in the quarter-final. Franz Beckenbauer's
Bayern Munich were defeated in the semi-final to set
up a clash with the Russians in Barcelona.

Having already lost two European finals, in 1961 and 1967, they were determined not to falter at their third attempt. By half time, they appeared to be on easy street. A terrific finish from Colin Stein and a Willie Johnston header had put Rangers 2-0 up. Within a few minutes of the second half starting, Johnston latched on to a Peter McCloy goal-kick and made it three. The match should have been dead and buried.

Jubilation at the final whistle

But on the hour mark, Vladimir Eshtrekov pulled one back for Dynamo and made the Scots nervy. With just three minutes left Aleksandr Makhovikov made it 3-2 and the hordes of Scottish fans in the stadium thought Rangers had blown it.

But they hung on to record a memorable victory and those jubilant supporters invaded the pitch at full time. It was an outpouring of emotion after the disaster just 17 months before. They had also matched arch-rivals Celtic in winning a European trophy.

But the invasion meant skipper John Greig was presented with the trophy in a room within the ground and was unable to parade it in front of his own supporters – the one downside to a joyous evening.

Rangers:
McCloy, Jardine, Mathieson, Johnstone, Greig, McLean, Smith, MacDonald, Conn, Stein, Johnston

Scorer:
Johnston (2), Stein

Attendance:
24,701

LEEDS UNITED 1 RANGERS 2

Champions League qualifier, 2nd leg, Elland Road, 4th November 1992

Everyone had written off Rangers before a ball had even been kicked in the 'Battle of Britain' against English champions Leeds United.

Ally McCoist reaches the heights against Leeds

After defeating Danish side Lyngby in the first qualifying round of the inaugural Champions League, the Ibrox men were drawn against an Elland Road outfit boasting stars like Eric Cantona, Gary McAllister, Gordon Strachan and Gary Speed.

In England, Scottish football was regarded as second-rate and Walter Smith's team weren't given a hope of making it to the group stages.

Despite going a goal down in the first minute of the first-leg to a McAllister volley, Rangers recovered to secure a 2-1 win thanks to John Lukic's own goal and a trademark Ally McCoist strike. But when they arrived in Yorkshire for the return match, it was widely accepted Leeds would be too good for their Scottish counterparts. How wrong that was.

Only two minutes into the game, Mark Hateley latched on to a McCoist head-flick to send a magnificent 20-yard shot which flew past Lukic into the top corner.

With no Rangers fans allowed at the away leg, Leeds' famous old ground had been stunned into silence. The home support suddenly realised Rangers were the real deal.

Hugely influenced by French star Cantona, Howard Wilkinson's side pressed hard for an equaliser and a route back into the tie. But Gers' defence stood firm and was marshalled superbly by captain Richard Gough and John Brown.

They also had, arguably, Britain's best goalkeeper behind them in Andy Goram who, along with fellow Yorkshire-born team-mate Stuart McCall, were desperate to send Leeds spinning out.

As the increasingly desperate home side threw everything at Rangers, it meant there was space to hit them on the counter-attack. On 59 minutes Smith's men took full advantage to go 2-0 up and kill off the tie.

Hateley's back-heel found Ian Durrant whose return pass to the English striker sent him scampering down the left flank. He looked up and found strike partner McCoist with an inch-perfect cross and Super Ally's diving header gave Lukic no chance.

Cantona notched a consolation goal with five minutes left but Rangers emerged victorious to prove their doubters wrong.

Rangers:
Goram, McPherson, Gough, Brown, Robertson, Gordon (Mikhailichenko), McCall, Ferguson, Durrant, Hateley, McCoist

Scorer:
Hateley, McCoist

Attendance:
25,118

CELTIC 0 RANGERS 3

Scottish Premier League, Celtic Park, 22nd May 1999

There can be no sweeter feeling than winning the league championship at the home of your oldest and fiercest rivals. Rangers achieved that feat in 1999 when Dick Advocaat's side clinched their 48th SPL title, the first time in the club's history they had done so at Celtic Park.

Jorge Albertz had plenty to smile about...

It was the Dutchman's first season at Ibrox and his new brand of football – and multi-million pound signings – had re-energised Rangers and galvanised a support which had been distraught at the end of the previous campaign when Walter Smith's side had failed to win ten-in-a-row.

Advocaat's men arrived at Parkhead needing just three points against Jo Venglos' Celtic outfit to lift the trophy. No one could have predicted the margin of Gers' victory and the circumstances which surrounded a match immediately dubbed Scotland's "Shame Game".

Rangers took a 12th minute lead when Neil McCann steered a Rod Wallace cross past Jonathan Gould from six yards. But the real drama had yet to unfold.

After Celtic defender Stephane Mahe was ordered off by referee Hugh Dallas, the official suffered a torrent of abuse from the home crowd and an enraged Hoops' fan got on to the pitch in a bid to get at him.

... while for Vidar Riseth there was only misery

Coins had already been thrown towards Rangers players before Dallas was struck by one on 41 minutes, which resulted in him needing treatment to a head wound.

From a Rangers free-kick just seconds later, Dallas awarded a penalty to Advocaat's side for a push by Vidar Riseth on Tony Vidmar. The decision caused anger among the Celtic players and supporters who were adamant he had pointed to the spot as a direct result of being targeted by the Hoops fans.

Jorg Albertz scored the penalty to put Gers two-up and all but seal the championship. McCann scored a third goal in the second half to put the icing on the cake for Rangers' travelling support - before Dallas had to produce another two red cards for Wallace and Riseth towards the end of the game.

As if the day hadn't been bad enough for Celtic, the Rangers players mimicked their rivals at full-time by doing a 'Huddle' in front of the away end – a tradition their hosts had become renowned for.

Rangers:
Klos, Porrini, Amoruso, Hendry, Vidmar, Reyna, Van Bronckhorst, Albertz (McInnes), McCann, Wallace, Amato (Johansson)

Scorer:
McCann (2), Wallace

Attendance:
59,918

LYON 0 RANGERS 3

Champions League, group stage, Stade de Gerland, 2nd October 2007

Rangers' 2007/08 Euro campaign will forever be remembered for their charge towards the UEFA Cup final against Zenit St Petersburg – when a 2-0 defeat ended their hopes of lifting a European trophy for the second time in their history.

But earlier in the season, during their Champions League assault, Walter Smith's side pulled off one of their most remarkable results on the continent ever.

The Stade de Gerland was a formidable destination

Their 3-0 demolition of French champions Lyon sent shock waves around Europe and a clear message that the Ibrox club were a force to be reckoned with that season.

Rangers had began their Champions League group with a superb 2-1 victory over Stuttgart at Ibrox which set them up perfectly for their trip to the Stade de Gerland – where Lyon had already beaten some of the biggest names in world football.

In Scotland, the feeling was that if Gers could come

back from France with even a point it would be a massive result for Smith and his team. But they would return to Glasgow with far more than that.

In the 23rd minute, DaMarcus Beasley's corner was met by Lee McCulloch

Rangers' travelling support were delighted with what they saw

who rose to bullet home a header from close range. The goal stunned Lyon coach Alain Perrin but sent the travelling Bears wild with delight.

Rangers held on to their lead until half time, having survived a scare when Brazilian superstar Juninho rattled Allan McGregor's crossbar with a brilliant free kick.

But Smith's men weren't content to settle for a narrow victory. Just three minutes into the second half, Alan Hutton's cross found Daniel Cousin in the box and the big striker swivelled before rifling a terrific shot past Vercoutre to double Rangers' advantage.

The emphatic win was sealed on 53 minutes when Cousin's audacious pass from inside his own half was perfect for American winger Beasley who calmly took a touch on the run before slotting the ball home.

Ultimately, Gers would go no further in the Champions League and finished the season on a march to Manchester in the UEFA Cup.

But no one will forget the night they hammered Lyon in their own back yard.

Rangers:
McGregor, Hutton, Cuellar, Weir, Papac, McCulloch (Novo), Hemdani, Ferguson, Thomson, Beasley (Adam), Cousin (Whittaker)

Scorer:
McCulloch, Cousin, Beasley

Attendance:
38,076

RANGERS COMIC STRIP HISTORY

4

AFTER A SHOCKING RANGERS DISPLAY AT ST. JOHNSTONE, FURIOUS MANAGER GRAEME SOUNESS GAVE HIS TEAM QUITE A ROLLICKING...

THAT WAS ★@☆✕-!! RUBBISH! YOU SHOULD ★@☉!! APOLOGISE TO THE FANS!

VISITORS DRESSING ROOM

ST. JOHNSTONE'S TEA-LADY AGGIE MOFFAT CONFRONTED SOUNESS...

YOU ARE A RUDE, FOUL-MOUTHED MAN! AND LOOK AT THIS MESS...WOULD **YOU** LEAVE YOUR OWN HOUSE LIKE THIS?

DON'T TALK TO ME LIKE THAT, YOU SECOND-RATE CLEANER...

THE RANGERS BOSS COMPLAINED TO THE ST. JOHNSTONE CHAIRMAN ABOUT AGGIE, BUT IT WAS THE BEGINNING OF THE END FOR SOUNESS, LATER IN THE SEASON...

OFFERED FIVE YEAR CONTRACT

SOUNESS NEW MANAGER OF LIVERPOOL

HE LATER ADMITTED HIS SPAT WITH THE TEA-LADY AT McDIARMID PARK HAD HASTENED HIS DEPARTURE FROM IBROX...

THE RANGERS STORY
MODERN TIMES
1998-2010

Dick Advocaat was officially appointed manager of Rangers on 1st June 1998. It was a bold move by David Murray, signalling an intention to achieve European, as well as domestic, success. The Dutch coach had a glowing reputation after his time with PSV Eindhoven and the Holland national side. He had a new squad to build at Ibrox and Murray was willing to fund it.

In total, 15 players from the Smith era left the club that summer so Advocaat had to buy big. Dutch international stars Arthur Numan and Giovanni Van Bronckhorst arrived, as did Russian winger Andrei Kanchelskis, French keeper Lionel Charbonnier, English striker Rod Wallace and Scotland skipper Colin Hendry.

The £36.5 million Advocaat spent on players brought instant success as he won the treble. St Johnstone were beaten in the League Cup final, while Wallace's solitary goal at Hampden against Celtic in the Scottish Cup final clinched a clean sweep of trophies.

The title was sealed in the sweetest fashion before the Scottish Cup final win with a 3-0 drubbing of Celtic at Parkhead, making Advocaat a Gers hero.

The following year, another eight players left and players such as Michael Mols and Tugay were added to a squad which also included German goalie Stefan Klos and American playmaker Claudio Reyna. Incredibly, the championship was won by 21 points from Celtic and a 4-0 victory over Aberdeen in the Scottish Cup secured a double.

In Europe, Rangers were playing a style of football which hadn't been witnessed at Ibrox for years. A memorable win over Italian side Parma in the Champions League qualifier took Advocaat's men into the group stages where they came close to making the last 16.

A cruel injury to Mols against Bayern Munich wrecked their chances and they had to settle for a place in the UEFA Cup where they suffered a penalty shoot-out defeat to Borussia Dortmund.

Celtic recruited Martin O'Neill in 2000 in a bid to

Elation as victory in the 1999 Scottish Cup final seals another treble

Claudio Cannigia takes on PSG's Lionel Potillon in the 2001 UEFA Cup

halt Rangers' dominance. Murray and Advocaat's response was to spend a Scottish record £12 million fee on Norwegian hitman Tore Andre Flo from Chelsea. Ronald de Boer and Kenny Miller were also brought in but O'Neill claimed a treble in his first season at Celtic, leaving Advocaat under pressure. With his side struggling in the SPL the following year, he announced he was quitting after a memorable UEFA Cup penalties victory over Paris St Germain in France.

He would be replaced by a Scot, Alex McLeish, who was given the daunting task of stopping O'Neill in his tracks but with less money than his predecessor enjoyed. In the first six months of his reign, 'Big Eck' won the League Cup and Scottish Cup. In 2002/03, McLeish led his side to a treble – a remarkable achievement as the club continued to downsize.

The title was clinched in dramatic style on the last day when Gers had to beat Dunfermline by a bigger winning margin than Celtic, who were playing at Kilmarnock. With Celtic 4-0 up at Rugby Park and McLeish's men leading 5-1 at Ibrox, Mikel Arteta smashed home a late penalty to win the crown in unforgettable fashion.

McLeish still had little to spend and relied on free transfers such as Nuno Capucho and Egil Ostenstad. And with Celtic strong under O'Neill, it was no real surprise the Govan club finished the 2003/04 campaign trophyless. But they would savour unbridled joy in 2005.

In a last-day finish which matched 2003 for drama, Rangers defied the odds to win the league at Easter Road. Motherwell's shock victory over Celtic, after coming from a goal behind in the final minutes, meant Nacho Novo's strike against Hibs had secured another title.

Rangers couldn't retain the championship but made giant steps in Europe, qualifying for the last 16 of the Champions League. A 3-2 win over FC Porto at Ibrox and a 1-1 draw at home to Inter Milan, as well as two draws against Artmedia Bratislava and another point picked up in Portugal, took them through to the knock-out phase where they unluckily lost to Villarreal on away goals.

Rangers' SPL form was poor but, unlike Advocaat, McLeish had made £13.6 million in profit from transfer dealings and when he left Ibrox in May 2006, it was with his head held high.

His replacement was Paul Le Guen, another major coup by Murray as the former Lyon coach had an outstanding reputation. Sadly, the move was catastrophic. An early exit from the League Cup to St Johnstone didn't help and Gers' form in the league was patchy. After an infamous row with Barry Ferguson before a game at Motherwell, in which the skipper was dropped and stripped of his armband, the writing was on the wall for the Frenchman. His time ended early in January 2007 and Murray knew the

Mikel Arteta scores the crucial sixth goal against Dunfermline to clinch the 2003 title

only man to lead his club out of the mire was old
Ibrox warhorse Walter Smith, then manager of
Scotland. Smith made an emotional return to Ibrox
with Ally McCoist as his assistant.

Barry Ferguson lifts the
2003 league trophy

Smith's side won 11 of their remaining 13 SPL
games and astute acquisitions like David Weir, Kevin
Thomson and Ugo Ehiogu steadied the ship. In the
summer, Carlos Cuellar, Jean-Claude Darcheville,
Steven Whittaker and Lee McCulloch joined. In one
of the most enthralling seasons in Rangers' history,
they won both domestic cup competitions but lost
the SPL title on the final day to Celtic.

Rangers fans gather in Manchester's Albert Square before the 2008 UEFA Cup final

That paled into insignificance, however, as Smith led his troops to the club's fourth European Final. After being knocked out of the Champions League, they entered the UEFA Cup. Panathanaikos, Werder Bremen, Sporting Lisbon and Fiorentina were all defeated but Russian side Zenit St Petersburg –

bossed, ironically by Dick Advocaat and inspired by the brilliant Andrei Arshavin – deservedly lifted the trophy with a 2-0 victory.

More than 150,000 Rangers supporters travelled to the final in Manchester and violent exchanges with police in the city centre soured what had been a monumental achievement.

In season 2008/09, the SPL title was the main priority and with the additions of Pedro Mendes, Steven Davis and Madjid Bougherra, the Ibrox side were crowned champions for the first time in four years, following a 3-0 triumph over Dundee United at Tannadice. The double was sealed with a 1-0 victory over Falkirk at a sun-drenched Hampden Park.

As Smith's budget was tightened further, the odds were stacked against Rangers regaining their championship in 09/10. But as Tony Mowbray's Celtic side floundered, Gers took advantage.

The League Cup had been won in March against St Mirren at Hampden when – after Rangers were reduced to nine men – Kenny Miller flashed in a late header.

However, the best was yet to come and a second consecutive title was clinched with a Kyle Lafferty goal against Hibs at Easter Road.

IBROX DISASTERS

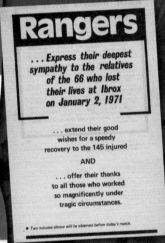

Rangers

... Express their deepest sympathy to the relatives of the 66 who lost their lives at Ibrox on January 2, 1971

... extend their good wishes for a speedy recovery to the 145 injured

AND

... offer their thanks to all those who worked so magnificently under tragic circumstances.

• *Two minutes silence will be observed before today's match.*

The darkest day in the history of Rangers Football Club came on Saturday 2nd January 1971 when 66 people lost their lives at Ibrox. Tragedy struck on Stairway 13 and from that moment, Rangers fans would be forever united in grief.

It was the afternoon of the traditional New Year Old Firm derby against Celtic and there were more than 80,000 supporters crammed into the stadium. The match was heading for a disappointing 0-0 draw when Hoops' hero Jimmy Johnstone scored in the 89th minute to send the Celtic faithful into a state of delirium.

For the Gers fans, it was despair. But there was to be a twist in the tale. With just seconds remaining Colin Stein hit a dramatic equaliser for the home side, causing huge celebration among the Rangers supporters. But that celebration was to be cut short with the tragedy that occurred seconds later at the back of the East Terrace.

It was originally thought that fans who were leaving the ground tried to turn back after Stein's leveller but a Fatal Accident Inquiry disproved that theory. There were simply too many people trying to get down the stairs at the same time and when some stumbled, suddenly a tidal wave of Rangers supporters engulfed them in a terrifying crush.

Artist's impression of the terrible scenes at Ibrox in 1902...

Such was the impact of the people trapped within the steel-reinforced fencing that ran down the sides of the stairway, preventing escape, that the barriers were left bent and twisted.

When the carnage had cleared hours later, 66 fans had died and more than 140 lay injured on the Ibrox pitch. Among the dead were 31 teenagers – the youngest victim nine-year-old Nigel Pickup who had travelled to the game from Liverpool. That was one of many harrowing stories.

Just one woman was among the fatalities. Margaret Ferguson, from Maddiston, near Falkirk, had made a doll for the baby daughter of Rangers striker Stein and had delivered it to his home just before Christmas.

Friends and family had gone to Ibrox together that day but would never see each other again. Five school pals from Markinch in Fife had travelled as part of the Glenrothes Rangers Supporters Club but never returned.

John Dawson was among the injured and said: "When the barrier gave way I was carried along a passageway for 20 yards with three people on top of me and at least three underneath."

Another survivor was Robert Black who remembers: "There was so much pressure from behind me that I was tossed down on top of others. People were on the ground and I was thrown over them. I was just carried forward by the surge."

There are indelible images of Rangers manager Willie Waddell and Celtic boss Jock Stein in the aftermath, helping to carry the bodies of those who didn't survive. Waddell vowed later that the club would have players and representatives at every one of the 66 funerals and he was true to his word.

Both sides of the Old Firm put aside their fierce rivalry to play in a game aimed at raising funds for the victims' families. A Gers/Celtic select took on a Scotland XI at Hampden which attracted a crowd of 81,405 people. George Best and Bobby Charlton made guest appearances.

On the 30th anniversary of the Ibrox Disaster a memorial service was held at the stadium and in honour of the victims a bronze statue of legend John Greig, who was captain that black day and who later managed the club, was unveiled above a plaque with the names of every fan who lost their life. And every year, at the home game closest to the anniversary, the club pays its respect by laying a special wreath at the statue.

To experience one major disaster is horrifying for any football club. But sadly, tragedy had struck Rangers twice before.

A decade earlier, two supporters died on Stairway 13 and 44 people were injured. In 1963 Rangers spent £150,000 on improvements to that part of the stadium, a significant amount of money at that time.

But it couldn't prevent further incidents, nor the horror of 1971.

The first Ibrox Disaster occurred on 5th April 1902 when the club hosted a Scotland v England international match.

After 51 minutes the wooden terracing, named the West Tribune Stand, partially collapsed partly due to heavy rainfall the previous night. Under the weight of so many spectators, a gaping hole opened up and fans plunged 40 feet to the ground.

... when a stand weakened by heavy rainfall collapsed, killing 25 and injuring hundreds

A total of 25 people died and 587 were injured but remarkably the game continued, with players and officials unaware of the events that were unfolding.

Following the disaster, the wooden terrace with steel frame design was discredited and Ibrox became a safer and more comfortable stadium.

The replayed Auld Enemy clash was played at Villa Park on 3rd May 1902, with the £1,000 proceeds from the 2-2 draw going to the Ibrox Disaster Relief Fund.

HONOURS AND RECORDS

MAJOR HONOURS

World record league title wins: 53
World record domestic title wins: 113
World record number of domestic trebles: 7
First club in the world to win 100 trophies

WINNERS

Scottish League champions 1891, 1899, 1900, 1901, 1902, 1911, 1912, 1913, 1918, 1920, 1921, 1923, 1924, 1925, 1927, 1928, 1929, 1930, 1931, 1933, 1934, 1935, 1937, 1939, 1947, 1949, 1950, 1953, 1956, 1957, 1959, 1961, 1963, 1964, 1975, 1976, 1978, 1987, 1989, 1990, 1991, 1992, 1993, 1994, 1995, 1996, 1997, 1999, 2000, 2003, 2005, 2009, 2010
Emergency War League champions 1940
Southern League 1941, 1942, 1943, 1944, 1945, 1946

Glasgow League 1896, 1898
European Cup-Winners' Cup 1972
Scottish Cup 1894, 1897, 1898, 1903, 1928, 1930, 1932, 1934, 1935, 1936, 1948, 1949, 1950, 1953, 1960, 1962, 1963, 1964, 1966, 1973, 1976, 1978, 1979, 1981, 1992, 1993, 1996, 1999, 2000, 2002, 2003, 2008, 2009
Scottish League Cup 1947, 1949, 1961, 1962, 1964, 1965, 1971, 1976, 1978, 1979, 1982, 1984, 1985, 1987, 1988, 1989, 1991, 1993, 1994, 1997, 1999, 2002, 2003, 2005, 2008, 2010
Emergency War Cup 1940
Southern League Cup 1941, 1942, 1943, 1945
Glasgow Cup 1893, 1894, 1897, 1898, 1900, 1901, 1902, 1911, 1912, 1913, 1914, 1918, 1919, 1922, 1923, 1924, 1925, 1930, 1932, 1933, 1934, 1936, 1937, 1938, 1940, 1942, 1943, 1944, 1945, 1948, 1950, 1954, 1957, 1958, 1960, 1969, 1971, 1975, 1976, 1979, 1983, 1985, 1986, 1987
Glasgow Merchants and Charity Cup 1879, 1897, 1900, 1904, 1906, 1907, 1909, 1911, 1919, 1922, 1923, 1925, 1928, 1929, 1930, 1931, 1932, 1933, 1934, 1939, 1940, 1941, 1942, 1944, 1945, 1946, 1947, 1948, 1951, 1955, 1957, 1960

RUNNERS-UP

Scottish League championship 1893, 1896, 1898, 1914, 1916, 1919, 1922, 1932, 1936, 1948, 1951, 1952, 1953, 1958, 1962, 1966, 1967, 1968, 1969, 1970, 1973, 1977, 1979, 1998, 2001, 2002, 2004, 2007, 2008
UEFA Cup 2008
European Cup-Winners Cup 1961, 1967
UEFA Super Cup 1972
Scottish Cup 1877, 1879, 1899, 1904, 1905, 1921, 1922, 1929, 1969, 1971, 1977, 1980, 1982, 1983, 1989, 1994, 1998
Scottish League Cup 1952, 1958, 1966, 1967, 1983, 1990, 2009

MINOR HONOURS
WINNERS

Rangers Sports Trophy 1890
Glasgow International Exhibition Cup 1901
Scottish National Exhibition Tournament 1908
Lord Provosts Cup 1921
British Championship 1933
Sir Archibald Sinclair Cup 1942
Summer Cup 1942
Scottish Victory Cup 1946
Paisley Charity Cup 1972
Jet Cup 1977
Tennent Caledonian Cup 1978
Drybrough Cup 1979
Dubai Champions Cup 1987
Forum Cup 1991

Ibrox International Challenge Trophy 1995
Wernesgruner Cup 2003
Walter Tull Memorial Cup 2004

CLUB RECORDS

Record win: 14-2 (v Blairgowrie, 20th January 1934)
Record league Win: 10-0 (v Hibernian, 24th December 1898)
Record Scottish Cup win: 13-0; v Possilpark, 6th October 1877; v Uddingston, 10th November 1877; v Kelvinside, 28th September 1889)
Record League Cup win: 9-1 (v St. Johnstone, 15th August 1964)
Record European win: 10-0 on aggregate (v Valletta, 28th September 1983)
Most league goals scored in a season: 118 in 38 games (1933/34)
Record transfer fee paid: Tore Andre Flo, £12,000,000 (from Chelsea, 23rd November 2000)
Record transfer fee received: Alan Hutton, £9,000,000 (to Spurs, 30th January 2008)
Most points in a season: (2 points for a win) 76, 1920/21; (3 points for a win) 97, 2002/03
Fewest points in a season: (2 points for a win) 20, 1893/94; (3 points for a win) 69, 1994/95
Record league attendance: 118,567 v Celtic, won 2-1, Ibrox Park, 2nd January 1939

Record Scottish Cup attendance: 143,570 v Hibernian, won 1–0, Hampden Park (N), 27th March 1948

Record League Cup Attendance: 125,154 v Hibernian, won 3–1, Hampden Park (N), 22 March 1947

INDIVIDUAL RECORDS

Most appearances: John Greig, 755 (1961-1978)

Most Scottish League Cup appearances: John Greig, 121 (1961-1978)

Most Scottish League appearances: Sandy Archibald, 513 (1917-1934)

Most Scottish Cup appearances: Alec Smith, 74 (1894-1915)

Most European appearances: Barry Ferguson, 82 (1994-2003, 2005-2009)

Youngest first-team player: Derek Ferguson, 16 years, 24 days (v Queen of the South, 24th August 1983)

Oldest first-team player: David Weir, 39 years, 364 days (v Motherwell, 9th May 2010)

Oldest debutant: Billy Thomson, 37 years, 50 days (v Dundee United, 1st April 1995)

Most consecutive appearances: William Robb, 241 (13th April 1920 – 31st October 1925)

Most appearances in a season: Carlos Cuéllar, 65 (2007/08)

Longest-serving player: Dougie Gray, 22 years (27th July 1925 – May 1947)

Most goals in all competitions: Ally McCoist, 355 (1983-1998)

Most Scottish League goals: Ally McCoist, 251

Most Scottish Cup goals: Jimmy Fleming, 44

Most League Cup goals: Ally McCoist, 54 (right)

Most European goals: Ally McCoist, 21

Most goals in one season: Jim Forrest, 57 (1964-65)

Most League goals in one season: Sam English, 44 (1931-32)

Most hat-tricks: Ally McCoist, 28

Most penalties scored: Johnny Hubbard, 54

Youngest goalscorer: Derek Johnstone, 16 years, 319 days (v Cowdenbeath, 19th September 1970)

Oldest goalscorer: David Weir, 38 years, 183 days (v Kilmarnock, 9th November 2008)

INTERNATIONAL RECORDS

Most international caps while a Rangers player: Ally McCoist, 59 (Scotland)

Most capped player to play for Rangers: Frank de Boer, 112 (Holland)

Most capped Scottish player to play for Rangers: Christian Dailly, 67

Most international goals while a Rangers player: Ally McCoist, 19 (Scotland)

Most World Cup appearances while a Rangers player: Sandy Jardine, 4 (Scotland)

Most World Cup goals while a Rangers player: Sammy Baird (Scotland), Mo Johnston (Scotland) 1

Most European Championship appearances while a Rangers Player: Andy Goram, Stuart McCall, 6 (Scotland)
Most European Championship goals while a Rangers player: Brian Laudrup, 3 (Denmark)

SPFA PLAYER OF THE YEAR AWARDS

1977/78: Derek Johnstone
1991/92: Ally McCoist
1992/93: Andy Goram
1993/94: Mark Hateley
1994/95: Brian Laudrup
1995/96: Paul Gascoigne
2001/02: Lorenzo Amoruso
2002/03: Barry Ferguson
2004/05: Fernando Ricksen (joint winner)
2009/10: Steven Davis

SPFA YOUNG PLAYER OF THE YEAR AWARDS

1979/80: John MacDonald
1986/87: Robert Fleck
1994/95: Charlie Miller
1998/99: Barry Ferguson

SPFA MANAGER OF THE YEAR AWARDS

2009/10: Walter Smith

SPWA PLAYER OF THE YEAR AWARDS

1965/66: John Greig
1971/72: Dave Smith

1974/75: Sandy Jardine
1975/76: John Greig
1977/78: Derek Johnstone
1988/89: Richard Gough
1991/92: Ally McCoist
1992/93: Andy Goram
1993/94: Mark Hateley
1994/95: Brian Laudrup
1995/96: Paul Gascoigne
1996/97: Brian Laudrup
1999/00: Barry Ferguson
2002/03: Barry Ferguson
2007/08: Carlos Cuellar
2009/10: David Weir

SPWA YOUNG PLAYER OF THE YEAR AWARDS

2009/10: Danny Wilson